I0818842

PLANT MAGIC

PLANT MAGIC

Enchanting Botanicals
to Enhance Your Life

CASSANDRA EASON

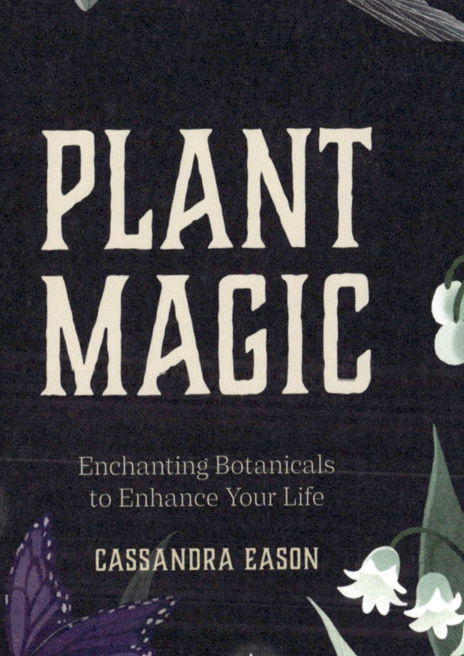

STERLING ETHOS
New York

Cover design by Stacy Wakefield Forte
Cover and chapter opener art by Eleanor Taylor

Sterling Ethos
Hachette Book Group
1290 Avenue of the Americas, New York, NY 10104
unionsquareandco.com
@unionsqandco

First Edition: May 2026

Sterling Ethos is an imprint of Grand Central Publishing, a division of Hachette Book Group, Inc.
The Sterling Ethos name and logo are registered trademarks of Hachette Book Group, Inc.

For additional picture credits see page 143

Print book interior design by Stacy Wakefield Forte

Library of Congress Cataloging-in-Publication Data is available upon request.
Library of Congress Control Number: 2025041317

ISBNs: 978-1-4549-9912-6 (hardcover), 978-1-4549-9913-3 (ebook)

Printed in China

1010

10 9 8 7 6 5 4 3 2 1

TO MY BELOVED CHILDREN,
TOM, JADE, JACK, MIRANDA,
AND BILL, AND MY BEAUTIFUL
GRANDCHILDREN, FREYA,
HOLLY, OLIVER, AND SOPHIE.

CONTENTS

INTRODUCTION

Flowers, trees, and culinary and medicinal herbs have formed the basis of the magical practices of both wise men and women and ordinary families worldwide since time immemorial. Many magical and healing remedies date from ancient Egyptian or Greek books of wisdom and have been collected by medieval healers and botanists. Others have been passed down through families for many generations, sometimes transported to other lands as seeds or cuttings by explorers and settlers across oceans or by migrating birds.

The knowledge I have collected over forty years or more that forms the basis of this book is a starting point for you that will evolve the more you explore the magical world of plants. *Plant Magic* explores traditional and modern methods of using plants to enhance daily life, attract positive outcomes—like love, health, and success—and shield against negative influences. You'll learn how to create sacred natural spaces, refreshed by the elements, to empower your magic.

Each section of the book is self-contained and offers information, suggestions, empowerments, enchantments, and rituals to add to the effectiveness and enjoyment of your garden, whether indoors or outdoors, and to increase your own abilities to manifest what you most need. Alternatively, you can dip into sections of the book for reference that are of most relevance to a particular purpose.

Remember, it is possible in the smallest of spaces to create a garden of plants that attracts love, prosperity, healing, protection, and well-being. Alternatively, you can find places where the relevant plants grow that you can make your own. Local parks and city squares often have gardens free for you to enjoy whenever the mood strikes you. Let the world rush by and fill yourself with the beauty of your favorite plant—connecting with perhaps the oldest form of wisdom known to humankind—receiving its ongoing power and blessings.

Lavender

1

THE WONDERFUL LANGUAGE OF FLOWERS

THE PRESENCE of flowers is life-enhancing—they transmit vitality and energy through their color and fragrance. Each individual flower also has a particular symbolism or energetic correspondence that can be harnessed for specific purposes.

For example, roses are popular key ingredients in love spells, whether grown from the earth for a garden ritual or cut and placed in a pot that can be sent to the object of your affection with magical intention. Fresh or dried petals conjure the grounding properties of the Earth element, and when scattered they can release magical energies or mark an outdoor space for meditation and contemplation.

The meanings of individual flowers are based on traditional ones that have been adapted by modern practitioners. The language of flowers, or floriography, was popularized in Victorian times, but was first formalized as a system of communication, especially between lovers, in the early eighteenth century. Lady Mary Wortley Montagu is credited with sparking a craze for floriography in England in the eighteenth century. Lady Mary was living in Turkey with her ambassador husband in the 1710s when she discovered women using flowers and other objects to exchange coded messages.

Earlier still, during the time of Elizabeth I and James I in England, flower meanings were quoted in verse and Shakespearean plays: gillyflowers were seen as symbols of gentleness, cowslips of wise counsel, pansies of thoughts, flowering rosemary of remembrance, marigolds of increasing love, and lavender of healing anger. This flower wisdom traveled with the early settlers to the New World along with seeds and plants, and indigenous flowers were added.

Lavender

Working with the Language of Flowers

When you buy potted or cut flowers, you can choose specific floral meanings to neutralize unwanted vibes in the home and workplace, or imbue your space with specific energies. However, there is still a special significance when you send flowers that convey a certain meaning. It is even better if you include an attached card to fill the gift with your essence—even if the card is added by the florist if ordered online.

SENDING FLOWERS

Sending flowers is an excellent way of speaking what is in your heart if there have been misunderstandings between you and someone else, or if you are reticent about sharing your feelings.

Read through the list of flowers on pages 16–26 and decide which flowers come closest to what you would wish to say but perhaps find hard to outwardly express. If the person lives close by, you can deliver the flowers yourself for an even stronger effect. Decide in advance what you want to say to the recipient via the flowers and incorporate the meaning as well as the message on the card. Afterward, buy one or two of the same kind of flowers you sent or gave to the person, and display them prominently in your home.

To fill your flowers with the essence of your message, hold your fingers together and your palms flat, facing toward and a few centimeters from your flowers. Repeat the messages you wish to convey slowly, over and over again, whether silently in your mind or out loud if you're alone, and they will be psychically transferred to the flowers that are to be sent.

If ordering online, call the flowers up on the screen, enlarge the image, memorize the look of the flowers, and then close your eyes and open them. For even more power, make an enlarged printout and set that flat on the table so you can move your hands over it. When you feel the connection, allow your hands to "type" your chosen message over the screen or printout as you recite it.

You may discover as you type that you have expanded your intention beyond the basic meaning of the flower. The way psychic energy flows is often compared to how information travels through the internet or digital waves. Both seem to operate on invisible channels, transmitting thoughts, emotions, and even intentions across distances.

Iris

A DIALOGUE OF FLOWERS

When you send flowers to a lover, family member, or close friend—either actual flowers or, if you wish, computer images of flowers via email or text—you can also share the meaning of the flowers to initiate an ongoing dialogue. This is a great way to stay connected if you need to keep your love private, can't meet often, or wish to keep conversations meaningful instead of getting lost in everyday small talk.

MORE FLOWER SIGNIFICANCE

The appearance of the flower also carries significance. For example, buds are symbols of new or early love. A flower in full bloom indicates commitment or strong feelings or wishes. A fully grown flower speaks to a matter that is settling and coming to fruition. A bouquet should contain all three stages of love.

If a flower is being offered to a friend or love interest, the way it is given is also full of meaning:

* A single flower offered on a leafless stem, flower uppermost, expresses the positive feelings and intentions of the giver.
* A flower surrounded by leaves or with thorns or prickles remaining, offered upright, conveys uncertainty that the love or positive message is returned.
* If the recipient inverts the flower and hands it back to the giver, they're equally uncertain but not entirely rejecting the overture.

- If the recipient removes any thorns that were on the flower and returns it upright, there is hope.
- However, if the leaves are removed from the stem and the flower is returned inverted, there will not be a positive outcome to the message.
- Small flowers refer to sensitive matters, early stages, or sometimes hidden factors. Medium-sized flowers stand for open, clear messages that can be shared. Tall flowers are for major issues that may stand out from the subsidiary messages.

Flowers & Their Meanings

The following listed meanings come from a variety of sources where there is general agreement on the significance of each flower. I have suggested a sample message for each flower, but you can adapt these according to your own specific purpose in sending or displaying the flowers.

ACACIA: Secret love; optimism; making friends: *Though none may know of our love, my heart is yours.*

AFRICAN VIOLET: House moves; bringing increased wealth and happiness: *Every happiness in your new life.*

ALYSSUM: Increasing what is of worth, whether love, money, or fulfillment: *I send you my wishes that your fortunes may continue to grow in the way you most desire.*

AMARANTH: Faithful love; beauty: *You are beautiful, and I pledge you my eternal devotion.*

AMARYLLIS: Achievements, especially in writing and all creative arts: *Your creative talents will soon find the recognition they deserve.*

ANEMONE: Calling a lost love back: *I miss you in my life and long to see you again.*

APPLE BLOSSOM: Fertility; good fortune: *May we soon see our desired infant in our lives.*

ASTER: Delicate matters or negotiations: *Let us talk so we can resolve our differences.*

AZALEA: Moderation; freedom from addiction: *Let us take our relationship more slowly, as I feel overwhelmed.*

BEE ORCHID: Putting right misunderstandings: *Let me explain and resolve what was a misunderstanding.*

BEGONIA: Protection against gossip; love that faces opposition; housewarming: *Nothing shall stand in the way of our love.*

Amaranth

BLUEBELL: Constancy and faithfulness: *Each year as the bluebells return is a reminder of my faithfulness to you.*

BUTTERCUP: Increasing wealth; sharing resources: *Whatever is mine, however little, I offer to you.*

CAMELLIA: Courage; desire: *Have courage and respond to my desire for you.*

CAMPION: Hidden passion; forbidden love: *Though others try to keep us apart, yet shall we not be parted.*

CARNATION (PINK): Being made welcome; acceptance into a family or work environment: *Welcome to our family.*

CARNATION (RED): Passion; also calling a love that is absent: *I miss you every day.*

CARNATION (WHITE): Maternal love; love in later years; truth: *This later love is doubly precious because we have waited.*

CARNATION (YELLOW): Protection against spite, envy, and the evil eye: *Do not let anyone come between us through jealousy.*

CELANDINE: Future happiness; gentle pleasure and vacations: *Come on vacation with me.*

Bluebell

CHRYSANTHEMUM (BROWN): Ending a relationship with kindness; healing animals: *I send healing to your beloved pet.*

CHRYSANTHEMUM (RED): Passion; also marriage: *Will you marry me?*

CHRYSANTHEMUM (WHITE): Truth and integrity: *Believe me, I would never lie to you.*

CHRYSANTHEMUM (YELLOW): Banishing gently an unwanted lover or a love gone cold: *Let us still be friends even though we are no longer lovers/partners.*

CORNFLOWER: Protecting the vulnerable; fertility and justice: *May you get justice from this unfair accusation.*

Daffodil

COWSLIP: Learning and examinations; wise advice: *Every success in your examination/test.*

CROCUS: Children and young people; joy; new beginnings: *Let us unite our families and share our lives.*

CYCLAMEN: Protection, especially psychic defense; endings leading to beginnings: *Though it cannot be the same between us, it can be better than before.*

DAFFODIL: Forgiveness; finding one true love: *I am truly sorry; you are my only love.*

DAHLIA: Change; travel: *Will you travel with me and face change together?*

Forget-me-not

DAISY (FIELD): First love; expanding the realms of possibility: *Believe in yourself and everything becomes possible.*

DAISY (MICHAELMAS): Seeking justice; anything to do with the fall: *You have achieved so much; keep faith with yourself.*

DANDELION: Wishes for the future; courage: *Your wishes will come true, and I will help fulfill them.*

DELPHINIUM: Getting the job you want: *Good luck with your job / your interview / the first day in your new career.*

EDELWEISS: Adventures; fun; moving far from home: *May your life be filled with excitement and adventure.*

EVENING PRIMROSE: Overcoming jealousy: *Do not let envy stand in the way of your happiness.*

FORGET-ME-NOT: Calling a lover who has gone away and is not in contact: *Do not forget me or what was between us and could be again.*

GARDENIA: Increasing beauty and radiance: *You grow more radiant every day.*

GERANIUM (PINK): Overcoming uncertainty: *Do not doubt me or my sincerity and loyalty.*

GERANIUM (RED): Commitment in love: *I pledge my heart to you.*

GILLYFLOWER/STOCK: Family joy; gentleness: *May the forthcoming family celebration you are working so hard to organize be filled with peace and happiness.*

GLADIOLUS: Strength, especially of character: *Stick to your principles. I will support you.*

GUELDER ROSE: Older people; winter matters: *Congratulations on this milestone birthday/anniversary. May you/we enjoy many more years of health and happiness.*

HAREBELL: Hope; restoration of trust: *Trust me. I will never again let you down.*

HEATHER (PINK): Good luck: *May you have good fortune come/return to your life.*

HEATHER (PURPLE): Faithfulness forever; success in money and gambling: *A lucky token to bring money and lasting good fortune to you.*

HEATHER (WHITE): Wishes manifested: *May your dearest wishes come true.*

HIBISCUS: Gentleness and healing: *May your health improve soon, and may you experience lasting healing.*

HOLLYHOCK (RED, PINK, AND YELLOW): Fertility; happy family life: *Welcome to the new addition to your family.*

Gladiolus

HOLLYHOCK (WHITE AND PURPLE): Altruistic ambitions: *I admire the good you do for others. The world needs more people like you.*

HONESTY: Integrity; financial advantage: *May your financial dealings soon bear lasting fruit.*

HONEYSUCKLE/WOODBINE: Domestic happiness; babies and children; love between siblings; protection from outside intrusion: *I send this as a token of my affection for you,* [name of sibling], *hoping we will soon be together.*

HYACINTH: Regaining lost love: *Let our love be rekindled and obstacles and opposition fade away.*

HYDRANGEA: Changing career; retirement; being laid off or resigning from the workplace: *Every success in your new job / study / life path.*

IRIS: Receiving long awaited news; mending quarrels; sympathy on the death of a long-standing life partner: *Sending you every sympathy and thoughts at this time of your grievous loss.*

JASMINE: Making dreams come true; discovering the identity of a secret admirer: *Now that I know your feelings, I ask you give me more signs.*

Hollyhock

JONQUIL: Encouraging mutual love; justice, especially personal; clearing up misunderstandings: *I would like to know you better.*

LAVENDER: Gentle love; healing: *I send you healing that your pain/sickness/ sorrow shall be lifted.*

LILAC: Domestic happiness; permanent relationships: *Welcome home. You have been greatly missed.*

LILY: Spiritual matters; marriage; mothers: *To my mother/grandmother with thanks on your special day or with special wishes for the love you always show me.*

Magnolia

LILY (TIGER): Wealth; achievements: *My achievements and possessions I will gladly share with you.*

MAGNOLIA: Beauty; sensuality; love of nature; nobility: *You are beautiful and of great worth.*

MARIGOLD: Marriage; money; employment; justice; summer matters: *Justice shall be ours at last.*

MIMOSA: Riches; increasing beauty: *One day we will be rich in money as well as love.*

NARCISSUS: Self-esteem; self-confidence: *Believe in yourself, for I believe in you.*

Nasturtium

NASTURTIUM: Victory; success; generosity; maternal devotion: *Thank you for believing in me when no one else did.*

OLEANDER: Wise caution, especially with money: *Beware those who are draining you of money with flattering words.*

ORANGE BLOSSOM: Marriage; fertility; abundance; health: *May your life be filled with health, happiness, love, and abundance.*

ORCHID: Perfection; overcoming rivals; prosperity: *None can equal you in my eyes and thoughts.*

PANSY: Togetherness; people from the past returning; kind thoughts: *I would welcome you in my life once more.*

PASSIONFLOWER: Finding a twin soul: *You are my soul mate.*

PEONY: Forgiveness: *I am sorry I spoke thoughtlessly. I did not mean my words.*

PERIWINKLE: Early love; memories: *Remember the happy times we shared.*

PETUNIA: Overcoming despair, debts, or fear; bringing calm: *All shall be well; do not lose hope.*

POINSETTIA: Unexpected gifts or offers; the return of light after the winter or a difficult life period: *Better times are coming soon, when life will go our way once more.*

POPPY: Peace; pleasure; increasing imaginative gifts; quiet sleep and dreams: *May you have beautiful dreams. I'll see you in my dreams.*

PRIMROSE: New love; spring matters; new beginnings: *Let us take this chance to start again.*

ROSE (PINK): First love; healing; a lover too shy to speak of their love: *You are my first true love.*

ROSE (RED): Love forever; health: *I will love you forever.*

ROSE (WHITE): Secret love; all secrets: *Tell no one what we share or what I have shared with you.*

ROSE (WILD): More uncertain affection: *I love you from afar.*

ROSE (YELLOW): Repelling jealousy; an older lover or love in later years: *Let us share our golden years. Reassure me, for I am afraid your attention strays from me.*

SNAPDRAGON: Overcoming rejection and loss; the revelation of truth: *At last you know the truth that my intentions were honorable.*

SNOWDROP: New beginnings; all matters concerning the spring: *Today is a new phase in our relationship, and the past is forgotten.*

Yellow Rose

SUNFLOWER: A wealthy lover; fulfillment of ambitions; splendid opportunities: *At last you have succeeded and will go from strength to strength.*

SWEET PEA: Partings; passion fulfilled: *Though we must part for a while, I hold you close in my heart.*

TULIP (PINK OR WHITE): Finding the perfect lover: *You are my ideal love.*

TULIP (RED): Love acknowledged: *What we share is special and eternal.*

TULIP (YELLOW): Unrequited love: *I love you in vain; do not reject me.*

Sunflower

VERONICA: Healing; recovery from illness; house moves: *I send you the healing of the angels for your swift recovery.*

VIOLET: Trust; modesty; keeping secrets: *We cannot speak openly of our love, but one day all will know and rejoice.*

WALLFLOWER: Happiness after misfortune: *There is a way for us to make a life together, and we shall follow it.*

WISTERIA: Breaking possessiveness that is holding you back; love and appreciation: *I will break free so we can be together.*

Flowers for Your Magical Celebration

From the earliest times, flowers have been an integral part of celebrations and commemorations from cradle to grave. They have been given, received, or planted for births, weddings, handfastings or commitment ceremonies, and anniversaries, a powerful life force infusion right through to death, where they have come to symbolize immortality and rebirth. In ancient Egypt, Tutankhamun was buried with a collar of olive leaves, cornflowers, and poppies that were still perfectly preserved when the tomb was opened in 1922.

Gifts of flowers play a significant role in the lives of ordinary people as a symbol of thankfulness and devotion to family members, as well as being offered in romantic love. For example, Mothering Sunday has been held on the fourth Sunday of Lent in the UK since the Middle Ages. On this holiday, Christians go to worship at the church of their baptism—their "Mother" church. Servant girls were given the day off and would gather wildflowers, such as violets and hedgerow flowers, from fields along country lanes on the way home. They would give these posies to their mothers as part of the

Wildflowers

tradition. This custom of flower-giving, which may even date back to pre-Christian times, continues today with the observation of the modern holiday of Mother's Day.

Mother's Day, observed in the US—and now in many other countries around the world—on the second Sunday in May, was founded by Virginia-born Anna M. Jarvis. Anna was determined that the life of her mother, who died on May 9, 1905, should be honored, along with that of other mothers who had died and perhaps had not been fully appreciated during their lives. White carnations, which have now become an integral feature of Mother's Day in many lands, were chosen by Anna because they were her mother's favorite flowers. They became linked with mothers who have passed over. In time, red carnations became the symbol of a living mother. Many people, however, choose their own mother's favorite flowers to give or send on Mother's Day.

WEDDING, HANDFASTING, AND COMMITMENT CEREMONY FLOWERS

On pages 30–38, I have listed the most popular flowers for weddings, handfastings, or commitment ceremonies (for brevity in this section I have referred to them all as wedding flowers). Many people choose to add a favorite flower to their wedding day bouquet, one with meaning to their relationship—perhaps one that grows in their shared garden or the first flowers they received from their beloved on Valentine's Day.

For a formal wedding you may choose traditional flowers such as orchids or roses, and guests can scatter rose petals instead of confetti. White is still the favored color, but especially for beach or tropical weddings there may be exotically colored flowers growing close by that you can purchase.

Lily of the Valley

You may want to carry a single flower or adorn the wedding and reception venue with flowers. Some of the most popular flowers that have been traditional for centuries, such as lily of the valley—which formed the bouquet of Grace Kelly and were included in the wedding flowers of the late Princess Diana and the current Princess of Wales—are quite toxic, best in bouquets rather than as table decorations if children will be present. If your skin is sensitive to a flower, you may want to tie extra ribbons, gauze, and/or muslin around the bouquet, or use a special holder of natural materials.

If it is an informal ceremony or a handfasting, add flowering herbs to a bouquet, such as lucky marjoram, abundance-bringing oregano, or rosemary, which promises you will always be in each other's thoughts.

The bouquet is usually tossed over the shoulder after the ceremony to be caught by a guest to indicate they will be next to marry. In a handfasting, set a few flowers from the bouquet next to a tree to thank the guardians of the place. Alternatively, dry your bouquet and make a special potpourri or incense or preserve some flowers for a future couple to serve as their "something old" and transfer the happiness of your special day.

Though I have suggested seasons when the flowers grow naturally in temperate zones, in practice almost all flowers can be grown in hothouses in most regions most of the year, especially for winter weddings. However, if possible, include a naturally blooming local flower (local to the venue if overseas) to connect with the life force of your chosen location.

AGAPANTHUS: Also called the African lily • blooms early summer to fall • blue, pink, purple, white, often striped • for people who want to fix their own wedding if family is interfering • good also for centerpieces and venue decorations

ALSTROEMERIA OR PERUVIAN LILY: Called the lily of the Incas, though not true lilies • blooms in summer

AMARYLLIS: Blooms winter to early spring; may rebloom during the year • red, pink, white • symbolizes love that is unwavering, through all times and circumstances • ideal for weddings of older people or those who have experienced obstacles before the happily-ever-after

ANEMONE/WINDFLOWER: Blooms in spring, summer, fall, according to species • red, orange, yellow-green, white, blue, purple, red-purple, ivory, pink • for an old love returned or a love that has taken time to flourish and workplace romances

ANTHURIUM: Also known as the flamingo flower • blooms in summer, but can flourish all year in the right conditions • bright red, green and white • ideal for beach weddings and outdoor celebrations

BELLS OF IRELAND: Blooms in summer, fall • white • beloved in bouquets of those of Celtic origin, though the flowers are not native to Ireland • also used in St. Patrick's Day floral arrangements • best when bells are half open

BOUGAINVILLEA: Blooms in spring, summer, fall • white, orange, purple, fuchsia • in its larger forms used for decorating tables, flower arches, and a church, wedding venue, or outdoor ritual area, or as single flower bouquet • the petals scattered instead of rose petals in an exotic or tropical wedding • for a joyous wedding or commitment day

BROMELIAD (BLOOMING VARIETIES): Blooms year-round • each one will flower only once, representing the preciousness of the love being celebrated • ideal for beach or tropical weddings

CAMELLIA: Blooms late in the fall through early spring where it is warmer • white, pink, red, yellow, lavender • for everlasting togetherness in love and prosperity

Bougainvillea

CARNATION: Blooms in spring • white, pink, coral, red; sometimes dyed • sometimes carried by older people at their weddings, especially in white for truth and fidelity in love • ideal for boutonnieres

CELOSIA: Blooms midsummer to fall • vivid colors, particularly beautiful in blue, though white is popular; the spiked form, often partly magenta, resembles wheat, a powerful abundance and fertility symbol • represents eternal love • speaks of undying love because they survive long after other flowers have faded in the fall • for exotic or high-profile weddings, or those where fun is the key and there is entertainment or an evening event

CHEROKEE ROSE: Blooms early to late spring, early summer • white with golden yellow stamens • for love after loss • for returning to your family across the world for the wedding if you emigrated or made a major interstate move • for following the wedding customs of your indigenous culture

CHRYSANTHEMUM: Blooms in summer, fall • jewel-like colors, red for marriage if one or both of you already have children, white for love none can come between • to harmonize boutonnieres and bouquets • formal weddings

CLEMATIS, WEDDING DAY VARIETY: Blooms May to September • creamy white flowers, also in purple, plum, and pink • for a union blessed by the angels • for a couple

Celosia

who intends to travel or is undergoing a major relocation or taking an extended honeymoon

CRASPEDIA: Also known as Billy buttons or sun balls • blooms June to October • yellow pompom flower balls • for bouquets, boutonnieres, and table decorations • for good health • for a wedding day and marriage based on laughter and goodwill • harmonizing different family members or rivals

DAHLIA: Blooms midsummer to fall • red, pink, orange, purple, white • eternal love • pink and purple especially for the renewal of vows ceremonies and nonreligious but spiritual ceremonies

Dahlia

DELPHINIUM: Blooms in spring, early summer • baby or brighter blue, purple, white • fulfills the superstition that a bride should carry something blue for good fortune and fidelity through the years • double delphiniums for unity, especially if a couple works together in business

FREESIA: Blooms in spring, summer • pink, red, white, purple, yellow, orange, blue • for a happy transition to the next stage of life together • for outdoor and garden weddings

FUCHSIA: Blooms in spring, summer, fall • red, bright pink, white, violet, purple • for deep love and trust • for home weddings

GARDENIA: Blooms in spring, summer, fall • white • for harmony in the years ahead • for a couple moving into a first or new home together

GERBERA DAISY: Blooms in summer, fall • red, yellow, orange, hot pink, white • white for love between generations, especially the couple and their parents, who may have substantially helped financially

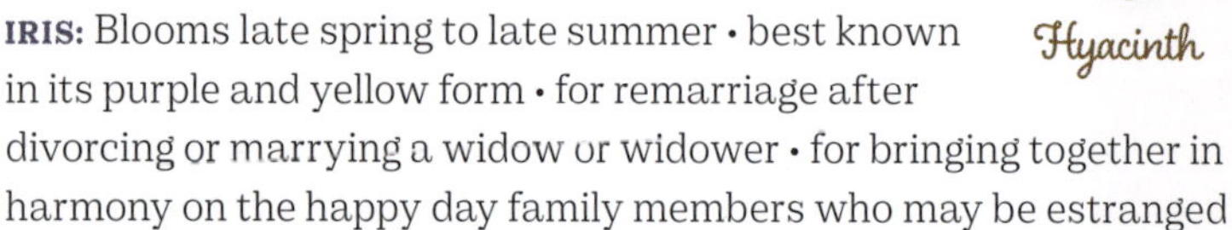

Hyacinth

IRIS: Blooms late spring to late summer • best known in its purple and yellow form • for remarriage after divorcing or marrying a widow or widower • for bringing together in harmony on the happy day family members who may be estranged

HYACINTH: Blooms in early spring • most popular in pink, blue, and white for early spring and Easter weddings • for a bride who lacks confidence in her beauty

HYDRANGEA: Blooms in summer, fall • most popular in white, pink, blue, and purple • formal and traditional celebrations as decorations or a single flower or the main flower in a large bouquet

LAVENDER: Blooms in summer • all shades of purple • to mend family coldness • for a first love, whether first time around or coming together years later • young love • if one of the partners is or has been sick

LILAC: Blooms in spring • purple, white • for weddings held at home or where there are many distant relatives gathering together • moving in together for the first time

LILY, CALLA OR ARUM: Not a true lily • blooms early summer to fall • especially in white or pink for weddings • myth says lilies were created from the Milky Way • calla lily for formal and traditional weddings, especially white weddings • remove stamens to avoid staining clothing

LILY OF THE VALLEY: Blooms in spring, but may vary according to location • white • present in many wedding bouquets • brings luck and happiness in love

LISIANTHUS: Blooms in summer, fall • often purple, pink, white • represents a lifelong bond between a couple who were friends for years before acknowledging love • for a garden or woodland wedding • in a wildflower or more formal bouquet

MADAGASCAR JASMINE: Often called the wedding flower • blooms spring to fall • white • symbol of wedded bliss • used for decoration as well as in a bouquet in formal or exotic weddings

MARIGOLD: Blooms in spring, summer, fall • especially popular in golden yellow, orange • for prosperity • after overcoming legal or financial wrangles with previous partners • because marigolds are associated with the Virgin Mary, for fertility where one or both of the couple have children but want more

Marigold

MIMOSA: Blooms early May to July • bright yellow • for love in later life, especially after former loss • lasting harmony

MUSCARI OR GRAPE HYACINTH: Blooms in early spring • most popular in clear blue, white, purple • featured in ancient Jewish weddings as decoration and a symbol of blessings upon the union

MYRTLE: Blooms in summer • white • made popular in wedding bouquets by Queen Victoria and subsequent royal brides, as a token of faithful, everlasting love

ORANGE BLOSSOM: Blooms in spring • white • sign of lasting love, fertility, prosperity, and good fortune • branches used as decorations as well as a bridal wreath

ORCHID: Blooms in spring (but obtainable all year) • white, green, orange, red, yellow, purple • a stately flower for a spiritual or religious ceremony, especially following family wedding traditions

PANSY: Blooms in spring, summer, fall • red, white, blue, yellow, orange, purple • colors often mixed in an informal bouquet for a garden or woodland wedding • used in bouquets tied with pink or green ribbons • for keeping the connection when one of the couple must travel or work away

Pansy

PEONY: Blooms late spring to late summer • white, pink, coral rose, red, purple • for larger celebrations • when a wedding planner has made a lot of the arrangements, used to keep the personal touch • brings blessings on all those present

PROTEA: Blooms late winter to early spring • pink, cream, white • some species have strong connections with weddings (e.g., blushing bride [*Serruria florida*] and other wedding-related names)

RANUNCULUS: Blooms February to August • yellow, pink, orange, purple, white • white especially used for boutonnieres, carried by flower girls, table decorations • mixed rainbow colors in a more exotic setting • add to garden roses and sweet peas for a country or garden wedding or a handfasting bouquet

ROSE: Blooms in spring, summer, fall • white, apricot, yellow, red, pink • picked wild for a handfasting, grown in the garden for a family celebration, or the finest hothouse blooms for a traditional religious or spiritual ceremony • often a mixture of buds through to fully grown for all the stages of love; the ultimate wedding flower • pink for young love • red for a twin soul • yellow for marriage in the golden years • white for a private ceremony attended by one or two friends or family members • best choice for boutonnieres and bridesmaid or flower girl posies (remove all thorns if home grown)

SNAPDRAGON: Blooms in spring, summer, fall • white, yellow, pink, orange, purple • white may be carried as the only or central bloom in a bouquet • ensures the day goes off without a hitch, especially if there are relatives who do not generally mix well

SWEET PEA: Blooms midsummer to fall, longer in some regions • purple, pink • for starting a new life together • for a large wedding where you do not know all the guests well

SUNFLOWER: Blooms summer to fall • golden yellow most popular • for fertility, abundance • sometimes carried at official parts of the ceremony and outdoor summer weddings

TULIP: Blooms in April and May, sometimes longer, depending on climate • all colors of the rainbow • pink and white for perfect love • red for private vows between an established couple • second or more marriages • renewal of vows

TWEEDIA: Blooms summer into fall • sky blue, white • another candidate for "something blue" for the bride as part of the bouquet • also used for decorations and boutonnieres • small, so not overpowering • signifying lasting happiness and harmony • very popular for DIY wedding bouquets

WHEAT/GRAIN: Grows later in summer and early fall • cream, brown, yellow, green • growing or dried plant with grains attached used for fertility, abundance, prosperity, and a secure home

Tulip

YARROW: Blooms in summer, fall • especially popular with yellow flowers, but also white, pink, red, purple, orange • an established feature of an informal bouquet, even if not flowering • represents fidelity, fertility • after the ceremony, can be dried and hung over the bed with other yarrow stalks and replaced every seven years

ANNIVERSARY FLOWERS

It is not certain when flowers were first exchanged by a couple on a wedding anniversary or sent as a gift by friends and family. It may have been as early as ancient Greek and Roman times. During the Middle Ages, maybe centuries earlier, a Germanic tradition existed where a husband would give his wife a silver wreath after twenty-five years of marriage and a gold one after fifty years. By Victorian times, anniversaries were formally recognized and flowers became a special token that had personal significance. Those who had little money would pick wildflowers, and many of these flowers are now cultivated in gardens and used in celebration bouquets.

The wedding bouquet is perhaps the most precious part of a marriage ceremony or handfasting because flowers, even cut ones, signify the life and growing love force between a couple. Symbolically renewing this love annually in flowers is a reminder that the love between a couple can thrive through any difficulty. Specific gemstones and materials have historically been associated with each anniversary; for example, the gem of the second wedding anniversary is the faith-pledging garnet, while the fiftieth anniversary is associated with gold. An anniversary gem or crystal can be hidden within an anniversary bouquet.

Often flowers that have meaning to the couple may be a re-creation of the original bouquet. Hanging baskets, especially if a beloved flower is a skin irritant, potted plants, and containers or plants for the garden are more lasting gifts and retain the living force within the flower even more powerfully than cut ones. If a beloved partner has died, you may take the appropriate flower to the gravesite on your wedding anniversary as a token of enduring love.

CHOOSING YOUR ANNIVERSARY FLOWERS

Unlike with gems and materials, there is less universal agreement about which flowers are associated with different anniversaries. While it is possible to obtain almost any flower from any part of the world at any season, you may prefer to buy plants that are grown locally in their own season, even in the depths of winter.

With the increasing popularity of the language of flowers from Victorian times, it may be possible to use the anniversary to convey a special floral message, repeating the meaning of the flowers in a written card. If you are presenting the bouquet yourself, you can hold it and endow it with special messages in advance as you picture the recipient.

· ANNIVERSARIES & THEIR FLOWERS ·

Some anniversary years do not have specific flower associations, and commercial gifts have often replaced more natural offerings. Where this occurs in the following list, I have marked with an asterisk a suitable anniversary flower based on the colors or themes associated with that anniversary. It is important to note that anniversary meanings, even official ones, can vary according to the source. In some years, where relevant, I have also listed two or more suggested flowers where there is customarily only one, so that you have a choice according to season and preferences.

1ST: Pansy, carnation

2ND: Cosmos, lily of the valley

3RD: Fuchsia, sunflower

4TH: Geranium, hydrangea

5TH: Daisy—larger cultivated variety, ox-eye daisy, African daisy, Gerbera daisy, Michaelmas daisy

6TH: Calla lily, balloon flower (bellflower)*

7TH: Jack-in-the-pulpit, freesia

8TH: Clematis, lilac

9TH: Poppy, bird of paradise

10TH: Daffodil, honesty (the mature, translucent, silvery disc-shaped seed pods)*

11TH: Morning glory, tulip

Daffodil

12TH: Peony, jade plant*

13TH: Hollyhock, any bright-colored chrysanthemum

14TH: Dahlia, pincushion,* laelia orchid

15TH: Crystal rose bush, white dittany

16TH: Bells of Ireland,* silver mound artemisia*

17TH: Canna lily, butterfly orchid*

18TH: Rose of Sharon,* love-in-a-mist

Iris

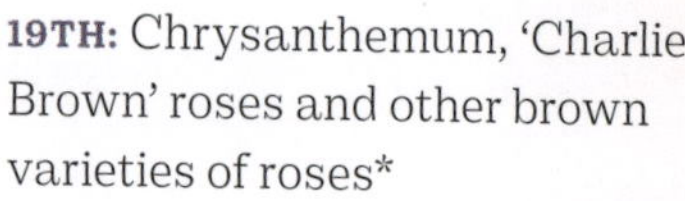

19TH: Chrysanthemum, 'Charlie Brown' roses and other brown varieties of roses*

20TH: Daylily, white asters such as the double-headed 'Boningale White', red roses

21ST: Azalea 'Golden Oriole',* marigolds*

22ND: Coppersmith cushion flower, burnt amber calla lily*

23RD: Treasure flower,* Mexican sunflower*

24TH: Flowering lavender, Canterbury bells*

25TH: Blue, purple and yellow iris, Buddleja 'Silver Anniversary'

26TH: Red roses, especially the 'Darcey' red rose

27TH: Cosmos in mixed colors, African violets*

28TH: Orchid, peace lily*

29TH: Celosia, other plumed or feathery plants such as goldenrod, amaranth*

30TH: 'Pink Pearl' rose, white lily, Choisya 'Aztec Pearl', Clematis 'Huldine' or Clematis 'White Pearl',* pearly everlasting

31ST: White lavender, any white flowers

32ND: Tweedia, forget-me-not*

33RD: Strawberry plant, pink zinnias*

34TH: Poppy, cornflower*

35TH: Any coral-colored flowers, such as coral roses, coral ranunculus, or coral snapdragons

36TH: Tea rose, pale pink carnations*

37TH: Thirty-seven small flowers in season, including a large red rose, baby's breath*

38TH: Flowers in season, a re-creation of the wedding bouquet*

39TH: Lace flower, gypsophila, anemone*

40TH: Gladiolus, *Astrantia major* 'Ruby Wedding', any ruby red flower*

41ST: Nasturtium in bright colors, orange germini (mini gerberas)*

42ND: Freesia, impatiens*

43RD: Sunflowers, tuberose,* petunia*

44TH: Flowers representing keynote events in married life,* magnolia*

45TH: Blue, purple and yellow iris, baby blue eyes*

46TH: Daffodil, mimosa*

Ranunculus

47TH: Camellia, *Astrantia maxima**

48TH: Purple New England asters, rose pink asters

49TH: Purple orchids, blue galaxy orchids*

50TH: Violets, yellow roses, clusters of the golden wedding Floribunda rose

51ST: Eryngo (sea holly),* delphiniums*

Lisianthus

52ND: Dahlia, bromeliad*

53RD: Cherry blossom,* delicate pale pink or white flowers in spring, at other times a mix of pink and white flowers*

54TH: Rhododendron, lisianthus,* dahlia

55TH: Calla lily, 'Stargazer' lily*

56TH: Box plant,* forsythia*

57TH: Yellow flag iris or Dutch iris,* azalea*

58TH: Maple tree leaves (representing balance, love, longevity, and abundance),* astilbe*

59TH: Olive tree leaves or blossoms, peace lily,* Easter lily*

60TH: 'Diamond Wedding' rose or other white roses

61ST: White orchids, such as northern lady's slipper orchid*

62ND: Mariposa lily,* hibiscus*

63RD: Lilac, lavender (*Lavandula angustifolia*) with silver leaves

64TH: Sunflower,* black-eyed Susan*

65TH: Alstroemeria (Peruvian lily),* blue hydrangea

66TH: Jasmine, flowers in all seven rainbow colors

67TH: *Stephanotis*,* star tulips*

68TH: Miniature citrus trees,* white garden hyacinth

69TH: Clematis 'Huldine' or Clematis 'White Pearl',* pearly everlasting

70TH: *Anthurium clarinervium*, peonies

71ST: Sweet pea,* any mixed colored flowers

72ND: Stock,* anthurium (flamingo flower or lily)*

73RD: Ginseng or ficus bonsai*

74TH: Candytufts, dianthus pinks

75TH: Champagne-colored roses, Dahlia 'Hamari Gold'*

76TH: Myrtle, either green or blooming white,* lily of the valley*

77TH: White ranunculus,* butterfly amaryllis*

78TH: Mixed pink, white, red, purple, and pink heathers, baby's breath

79TH: Mixed and bicolor pansies,* veronica*

80TH: Any item made of oak or oak leaves with acorns attached, tied with gold and silver ribbons*

Oak

A BOUQUET/POSY SPELL

Flowers can be incorporated into spells by empowering them with the significance you seek and enchanting them as suggested in the spell below. I made this three-flower spell for a woman I'll refer to here as Jenny many years ago, to help her overcome spite from her in-laws after her second marriage to a man we'll call Phil. Her new in-laws were being unpleasant to Jenny and her children because they had a strong bond with their previous daughter-in-law, even though she had been persistently unfaithful to their son and left him to be with her new lover, cutting all contact. Jenny was eager to make peace for the sake of her two young children, as her parents were no longer alive.

Like Jenny, you will need to do a little preparation and decide on the flowers you will be using for your spell, as many or as few as you wish. If you cannot obtain the flowers you want, you can substitute a similar color and kind that are in season.

Timing

Flower language spells work especially well when done in the morning. Unless you are an early riser, choose your flowers the night before and leave them in water overnight. If you have suitable flowers in your garden, you'll get the best results if you pick them just before the spell.

What You Will Need

* The chosen flowers, several of each kind if you want to make a nice bouquet to send or keep. Jenny chose yellow carnations to get rid of spite and unfair criticism, pink carnations for being made welcome by and accepted into Phil's family, and white canna lilies for a happy marriage and mothers because it was Phil's mother who was being especially unkind and trying to break up the marriage. If one need is predominant, you can increase the proportion or size of those flowers compared to the rest. You can, of course, use only one type of flower if you wish.
* A vase of water for the flowers.

The Spell

Take the flowers outdoors in the vase (you can work indoors if it's cold or rainy). Select one of the flowers. Jenny first chose a yellow carnation.

Hold the flower so that it rests in the palms of your hands. In this way energy can be transmitted via the small chakras in the hands, traveling into and from the plant. The flower energy filled Jenny with the power she needed to resist the negativity and unfair criticism, passing into the flower as a two-way exchange.

Speak words based on the energies of the flower—in Jenny's case, the yellow carnation to soften spite. You can create words linked to the flowers you choose and your needs. The more specific you are with identity of the intended recipient, the more focused the spell. Jenny's words were as follows:

Gentle carnation, shield me, my husband Phil and my children, Andrew and Penny, from the hurtful words and unkind actions of Brenda and Sean, my in-laws. May they replace anger with gentleness, malice with kindliness. As I count three, two, one, the spite is gone.

Next, take a second flower and rest it in your hands so it touches the first flower, then speak a few words about its energies. Jenny selected a pink carnation and brought it to the yellow carnation already in her hands, saying: *Welcoming pink carnation, make me and my children welcome in my in-laws' home and lives, so that Phil may likewise feel at home in his parents' home once more. As I count three, two, one, may harmony come.*

Finally, add a third flower and hold all three between your hands, adding a few words about what it represents. Jenny added one of the tall cream-colored lilies and said: *Lily of love, Brenda is a mother. I am a mother. We both love Phil. My marriage is precious and under threat. As I count three, two, one, the danger's gone. My spell is done. Let peace between our households come.*

Add more flowers of each variety and take them to your intended recipient, perhaps leaving them with a friendly message, as words from the heart are as effective as the finest poetry in a spell.

Jenny took her bouquet to her mother-in-law's house, leaving them on the doorstep. There were no miracles, but during the next weekend visit, Brenda thanked Jenny for the flowers, which she said were her favorites. Over the months, emotions softened, and when Jenny had a baby, relations thawed even more. Jenny repeated the spell weekly for a month, alternately keeping and sending the flowers to Brenda, and slowly the atmosphere softened.

2

CREATING A MAGICAL GARDEN

GARDENS CAN be created according to their plants and magical intentions to attract different strengths into your home, workplace, and life: prosperity and good fortune, love and fertility, healing, a happy home, the right plan-etary energies and enhanced psychic powers, particularly where plants are used as divinatory tools. In this chapter, we will discuss how to approach three different gardens that can be used to enhance your life.

Your Well-Being Garden

If you wish to grow plants with the intention of improving your everyday life—your stress level, your feeling of security, your good health, and more—a well-being garden is a great place to start. Every well-being garden has built-in protective powers—whether it is in an open space, a window box, or window ledges—which will guard the home, family, land, working environment, and pets against all harm. You can make a garden for your special needs or create a general well-being garden with separate sections, such as circular beds with the sections marked out by rocks, to represent needs such as prosperity or love within the garden. Indoors, you can place plants for specific needs in the appropriate spots in your home or workplace, such as money plants where you conduct business and pay invoices, and protective plants either just inside or on either side of the main entrances.

Your well-being garden is an ideal setting for creating a natural outdoor sacred space using plants that are refreshed by the wind and rain; your well-being garden is an ideal setting for this. You can make a sacred space indoors using potted flowers, greenery, and bonsai and tap into the ongoing restorative powers of nature to enhance and empower both informal spellcasting and more formal rituals.

On special festivals, invite friends and family to an outdoor celebration to which everyone contributes elemental plant gifts for the four quarters, such as patchouli for Earth and north, lemongrass incense for Air and east, basil or tarragon for Fire and south, and trailing greenery for Water and west.

USING YOUR WELL-BEING GARDEN

Most plants are multipurpose and can be dedicated and empowered when placed in soil or tended for the ongoing powers they offer as they grow. This multipurpose magical garden can spontaneously activate the qualities you and your family need at any time. The well-being garden is the ideal place to have a ready supply of plants to supplement your kitchen herbal jars and keep them fresh. You can take plants from your well-being garden to work in charm bags or as teas and so carry with you the money-making qualities you need; for example, mint can give you the courage to ask for an increase in salary.

The plants I have listed on pages 54–56 are all inherently protective for the home, family, and workplace. I have noted the plants with extra-powerful defensive strengths; they are helpful if you need extra support. As noted previously, you may want to divide your well-being garden into different areas for different purposes within the existing garden structure.

Pollen-rich flowers attract butterflies as well as bees, and these are linked with nature essences. Dragonflies, too, are considered spirit forms, and a small natural pond will draw them and their luck-bringing qualities to your garden.

PLANTS FOR YOUR WELL-BEING GARDEN

The following plants can be used in setting up a well-being garden indoors or outdoors for the first time or added to an existing garden, spread throughout in themed sections to allow positive energies to flow within the home, family, and workplace. By mixing these plants within a well-being garden, you ensure the ongoing intermingling of energies and that all their magical purposes continue to fill your life, home, and work.

BAMBOO: Immense good fortune • prosperity • marking the boundaries of your garden and life • protective from physical, psychological, and psychic harm • indoors as potted lucky bamboo plants tied with red ribbons on which may be tied a lucky Chinese divinatory coin

BAY LAUREL: Loyalty in all relationships • good fortune • health • attracting money • victory after a struggle

CACTUS: Fierce defense along boundaries or in the four corners indoors or outdoors against intruders and unhelpful neighbors and colleagues • survival in hard times

CINQUEFOIL: Asking favors • successful court cases and official matters • protection against debt • restful sleep

Bamboo

CUMIN: Protection against theft • preventing loss of what is precious in every way • peace of mind

GARDENIA: Healing • bringing peace • attracting new friends and lovers • calling good spirits into the garden

HONEYSUCKLE: Turning away doubts and fears and keeping safe family members who feel vulnerable • good against teenagers' friends who may wield an undesirable influence

LILAC: Protection of home • domestic happiness • calling home those estranged or far away

MARIGOLD: Justice • growing love • to gain admiration and to induce clairvoyance

MILK THISTLE: Maternal love • nurturing • protection against betrayal

Milk Thistle

PRIMROSE: Protection against adversity • uniting a family if children, teens, or new partners feel alienated • attracting and bringing awareness to nature essences

ROSEMARY: Fond memories of home • unity from afar

SAGE: Security • stability

SPEARMINT: Happy home • abundance in the home • healing

SUNFLOWERS: Happiness • success • granting wishes • honesty between family members • protection against scams

THYME: Long life • good health • older family members

VETIVER: Good fortune in the home • attraction of necessary resources • restoring calm after grief or loss • restoring tranquility in turbulent times

WILD GARLIC: Repelling harmful spirits • healing, especially when the white flowers are in full bloom

ESTABLISHING BOUNDARIES

Even in an existing garden it is important to mark out the boundaries of your protected and empowered well-being space.

- In hotter climates, plant a cactus at each of the four corners of the outdoor garden to protect the home from negative influences.
- Alternatively, outdoors insert nine bamboo canes at regular intervals inside your perimeter fence, surrounding each with a circle drawn clockwise in the earth. Tie scarlet cord from each of them, knotted nine times.
- If you have limited space outdoors, use wild garlic at the corners of the garden.
- In a colder place, use potted cacti, spiky green plants, or miniature bamboo

indoors at the four outermost corners of your home, office, or workspace.

- If you do not have a garden, plant a protective window box outside your apartment with cumin, rosemary, sage, spearmint, thyme, or any of the mints and vetiver or create a display in your kitchen of your favorite culinary herbs to use fresh in cooking.

SETTING THE SCENE

Here are a few easy ways to begin setting up your garden:

- If you bury a coin every week at the feet of a pottery garden gnome, it will ensure that money flows in and not out. Alternatively, create an outdoor sanctuary based around a stone nature spirit statue.
- Your well-being garden is the ideal place for creating a sacred workspace from a flat raised stone, a piece of wood resting on stones, or even a picnic table placed near the center of the garden or in your guardian spirit place (see pages 58–59). Indoors, position a low table surrounded by green plants where it will not be disturbed and where you can work magically.
- If a permanent sacred area is not practical, make a temporary working place near the center of your garden to dedicate and empower your garden, and then dismantle it with thanks afterward.

YOUR GARDEN (or Indoor Plant) GUARDIAN

Every garden—or, if you cultivate them, indoor plant—has a guardian spirit that can be discovered using the following process. You may already have detected this spirit in a clump of herbs, flowers, or a bush, though the energy may pervade the whole garden. Oftentimes, this location is the one to which you instinctively go to draw energy when you are tired or dispirited—that is indicative of the presence of a guardian spirit.

What You Will Need

A glass or crystal jug of gardening crystal water in which a gardening crystal has been soaked for eight hours.

Timing

Twilight or as dawn is breaking.

The Ritual

First, walk around the garden in silence three times in a clockwise direction, sprinkling water droplets from the crystal-infused water. Don't follow the shape of the garden; rather, focus on any especially significant or beloved plants.

As you do so, say in your mind continuously: *Guardian of this land, I seek to know you. I pledge to care for this place and would make you tribute.*

After the last circuit, return to the center of the garden and face the dawn or the dying light. Put down the jug and open your hands, palms up, arms bent, just above waist height. Say, *I ask now for a sign of your presence and your blessing.*

Keep walking around the garden, spiraling your footsteps until you feel connection beneath your feet or a tingling in your hands. This is your guardian's place. You may choose to locate or relocate your garden's natural sanctuary here.

In this natural sanctuary, you may detect a sudden movement or a flash of light, a bird call, a single brightly colored bird that swoops down, a brilliant butterfly or huge moth that appears and hovers, or occasionally a soft voice on a sudden breeze. The connection may manifest as a vibration in your hands and feet. Whenever you pick flowers or herbs, leave one in a dish for the guardian in their special place. In the guardian's place, also keep a very large unpolished green calcite crystal or a smaller round jade that will be washed by the rain, as well as a beautiful nature essence statue, a stone animal, a seashell, or a fossil. Keep the guardian's place swept and tidy, and it will form a source of personal power and healing of your garden.

MAKING YOUR GARDEN SACRED

To ready your space for ritual, contemplation, meditation, or just relaxing, here are a few tips:

* On your sacred work surface, place a bowl of dried herbs such as sage or thyme farthest away from you as you face the symbolic or actual directional north for the Earth element. Set it about halfway along the far side of the chosen surface.
* Burn a smudge stick in a container of sand or soil on the right side of the surface, again about halfway along, for your symbolic east and Air. Smudge sticks are dried and tied bundles of protective herbs. Use a small one indoors in a well-ventilated room. You can make your own smudge stick by tying together dried tall herbs such as lavender, rosemary, or sage, or buy them ready-made. If it is not safe to use fire or have embers possibly scatter, substitute a feather fan.
* Put a natural wax candle or garden torch in a deep heatproof container of sand or soil closest to you as you face the chosen place halfway along the bottom side for the symbolic or actual south and Fire. If it is not safe to have an open flame, use a battery-operated candle, a small charged solar light, or a red potted plant.
* Finally, place a dish of fresh water containing a gardening crystal, such as moss or tree (dendritic) agate, on the left side of the surface, again halfway along the side for your symbolic or actual west and Water element. Or use a trailing green plant.

- Gardening crystals include moss and tree agate; jade; green jasper; green, blue, or purple fluorite; green calcite; and rutilated quartz. Bury these beneath plants indoors or outdoors to revive them, or spiral a green crystal pendulum counterclockwise and then clockwise over the ailing plant to reawaken its life force. Keep a supply of gardening crystals in your special place.
- Place an offering dish in the center of the sacred space for flowers, preferably from the garden, which you replace regularly, or offer a dish of seeds such as sunflower or cumin to attract birds to your altar and garden. To the right of the offerings dish, set four gardening crystals in a small bowl.

DEDICATING AND EMPOWERING YOUR WELL-BEING GARDEN

To begin, visit the corners of your garden or indoor area, starting with the northwest corner. Bury a gardening crystal from the crystal dish in your sacred place in the earth in each corner, proceeding clockwise. While doing this, ask the nature essences living there to protect and bring life and growth to your garden. If working indoors, do this with four protective plants, one in each corner. Say for each *May you be blessed and bring blessings*. At each corner name any extra purposes for which you are dedicating your garden. Return the crystal dish to your sacred space and, moving from the sacred place again, scatter sage or thyme herbs around the boundaries of the garden or room, starting in the northwest. You should follow the shape of the garden or room.

At this point, light a smudge stick and move it naturally in clockwise spirals downward toward the earth and upward to the sky, as you walk clockwise around the garden or room boundaries, starting in the northwest and saying continuously, as a slow chant, *Powers of earth, our Mother; strengths of sky, our Father; enclose this place and make it a sanctuary of well-being.* Return the smudge stick to the sacred space and place it in a container. Carefully, with your broad-based candle, battery candle, red plant, or solar light, walk around the garden or room boundaries again, beginning in the northwest, saying *By Earth, Air, Fire, and Water, make powerful this sanctuary of well-being power and healing.* Return the candle to your sacred place. Then, taking the water bowl containing the crystals, sprinkle droplets of crystal water from the bowl on your plants with love as you pass around the boundaries of the garden or room clockwise, and again say *By Earth, Air, Fire, and Water, make powerful this sanctuary of well-being power and healing*. Extinguish the smudge and candle and tidy or dismantle your special natural place, saying *The ritual is ended, but its power and healing live and grow within this place. Blessings be on all.*

Once a week, make garden crystal water and sprinkle your boundaries clockwise, repeating *May you be blessed and bring blessings.*

Your Prosperity Garden

You can create a garden for prosperity using roughly the same format as your well-being garden. You may have even already planted prosperity herbs and flowers as part of your well-being garden. However, if money is an ongoing problem or you want to accumulate financial resources fast, secure a permanent source of income, or make the right investments, you can create a prosperity garden indoors or outdoors.

Alternatively, group your prosperity plants in a particular flowerbed within your well-being garden to call financial power at crucial times. Some of these wealth plants you may have already met in the book with other uses, for many plants are multipurpose.

You can empower your prosperity area when you plant or tend your flowers or herbs as you did for your well-being garden, but in this case as part of the empowering ritual, specifically name your current or future needs for money.

ENCHANTING YOUR PROSPERITY PLANTS FOR A SPECIFIC PURPOSE

As you choose and dry individual plants or groups of plants as part of your incense or charm bag (see page 102), you can give them extra power and direct the specific blessings you need by enchanting them. In times of specific need, you can also enchant your money herbs after or instead of empowering them (your choice) as they grow in the garden or on your kitchen windowsill to harness their power as they continue to grow.

You can use the same method for enchanting a specific plant or group of plants in a garden of love or for any other kind of specific magical garden, by adapting the words.

* Create a simple repetitive chant of four or five words highlighting the plant and its specific power, such as *Bergamot, bergamot, bring a profitable sale.*
* With your palms down, pass your hands a few centimeters above the chosen plant, moving your power or writing hand clockwise and the other counterclockwise at the same time in a slow rhythm while chanting your chosen words.
* Move your hands faster and speak the words faster. When you can feel the power building, slow down the movements and make the words likewise slower and quieter until they end in silence and you point both stilled hands vertically, fingers together, downward toward the chosen plant so you almost touch it. This will transfer and amplify the power for the specific purpose.

PROSPERITY PLANTS

AFRICAN VIOLETS: Indoor prosperity garden or area • soft fuzzy leaves and purple flowers signify wealth and growing prosperity in feng shui, especially through increased status

ALOE VERA: Indoor prosperity gardens or areas • increased income through good fortune • deters attacks from rivals

BASIL: Growing money by attaching Chinese coins to a strong growing basil plant • money incense • infusions poured down inside water outlets to stop money draining out

BAY LAUREL: Accumulating and conserving money • major purchases and investments • nine coins attached to a bay tree one a day for nine days and cast into flowing water on the full moon to call money by the next full moon

BERGAMOT: Successful property deals • encourages returns on investment and attracts fast money • wild bergamot outdoors and orange citrus bergamot outdoors in tropical or subtropical climes or indoors

BISTORT: Inflow of money in wealth sachets and in incense for instant resources for urgent or unexpected expenses

African Violet

CAMELLIA: Wealth and beautiful acquisitions • often the blossoms are used to bring luxurious living

CHAMOMILE: In prosperity charm bags to draw money • as a chamomile lawn to prevent financial loss

CINQUEFOIL: In prosperity mixes with a whole tonka or vanilla bean • protects against double dealing, deception, and financial scams

CLOVER/TREFOIL: Four leaves bring luck in financial affairs and wins in speculation, gaming, or lottery • five leaves attract hoped-for financial rewards • red clover encourages successful financial negotiations

Maidenhair Fern

FENUGREEK: Increasing prosperity over time, not only in resources but health and strength • seeds collected daily in a money jar for money spells

FERN (BOSTON AND MAIDENHAIR): Acquiring riches from an unexpected source • finding hidden treasure, indoors or outdoors

GINGER: In a garden or pot indoors grown to increase money supply • powdered root sprinkled into a jar of coins and shaken daily to speed up money inflow

MINT/PEPPERMINT: Instinctive awareness of a good vs. bad investment • money through overseas or online connections

MONEY TREE: Indoors as bonsai, with hand-like leaves, attracts money to the home and business through gifts, bonuses, and unexpected rewards

PATCHOULI: Ultimate money herb for all money and prosperity spells and mixes • where it grows, money will enter and stay

SAGE: Luck in games of chance • long-term prosperity through promotion and wise spending and saving • anti-shopaholic and anti-extravagance tendencies

CREATING YOUR PROSPERITY GARDEN INDOORS OR OUTDOORS

You can create a magical garden dedicated to prosperity if this is currently a major issue in your life. Often, however, it can form a section of a well-being garden as a separate flowerbed or area edged with stones or shells where you can work with plants dedicated to abundance and prosperity. After all, it is hard to focus on healing or love if money is an ongoing problem, so this may be an area to nurture to regularly keep abundance flowing into your life.

Just remember to not let it get overgrown or spill over into other areas, as this can represent money draining out or unduly affecting other areas of your life. Some other suggestions: If you are digging a new area—maybe replacing a wild area, lawn, or paved place in an existing garden—draw, in freshly dug earth, a large dollar sign or symbol of the currency of your own land and plant on top of it. Whether circular or square, which are good shapes for money-related needs, plant four money crystals: a tiger eye in the north, a citrine in the east, a turquoise in the south, and a lucky green aventurine in the west.

Choose from the plants previously listed in this section or any that feel right to you for full power. You can use the empowerment ritual on page 104, naming the specific purposes for which you need your money garden. If you prefer, move slowly counterclockwise for moon power, then clockwise for sun power, and then counterclockwise again for the moon power, saying as you stamp, step, and clap in a slow steady rhythm: *Guardians of this land as this garden grows, let abundance and prosperity rise, not fall, that there may be enough and more for all.* End with a final clap and stamp and leave a bowl of water in the center of the prosperity garden to absorb the full moonlight energies. The next morning, sprinkle the water at sunrise over your money plants, saying *Flow and grow by moon and sun, from this moment prosperity into my life will come.* Repeat the ritual on the next crescent moon once the waning moon has taken away all financial worries and obstacles to prosperity and a burrowing-in process and new financial success life is ready to grow. If you create your prosperity garden indoors, make a circle of your plants and put the bowl of water in the center to absorb the energies, even if the full moon cannot be seen.

KEEP WEALTH CIRCULATING AROUND YOUR LIFE AND HOME

Traditionally, magical gardens have near the center a glass fishing float, usually red, green, or blue and semi-transparent. These are often available from gift stores. Hang the float on a tree, bush, or sturdy post. Alternatively, use an oversized Christmas ornament or clear, unfaceted disco ball (or witch ball, as it is popularly called) through which you can see the plants to enhance the magical energies of your garden. This works especially well for amplifying money-growing energies.

In addition, you can see images reflected from within as the witch ball turns in the wind. This attracts prosperity and good fortune as well as health and protection. You can add to its wealth-growing powers by adding fenugreek seeds to it. This works at or near sunrise. If your ball has an opening, take the hook from the top of the ball and, through the hole, insert the seeds, saying slowly and continuously, *Fill all with your brightness, radiate your bountifulness, that abundance and wealth will grow and shine through my home all the year through*. When the ball is half full, hang it on a tree branch near the center of the garden or an ornamental branch indoors where air and light will circulate round it. Each time you pass the ball, swirl it nine times clockwise, saying *Nine by nine, make abundance mine.*

Your Love Garden

If love is a major issue in your life, you may want to devote your garden to it—although, as previously discussed, you can simply create a separate flowerbed within your well-being garden. If you don't have access to an outdoor garden, you can maintain a collection of indoor potted plants attuned to love. Whatever its form, a love garden attracts and enhances love if you are seeking romance or a partner, increases commitment in a hesitant lover, and stimulates or revives passion in a relationship that has become distant or routine. It can also preserve and increase family love among those within the home or far away by strengthening the telepathic love energy often not recognized or fully utilized.

Generally, even plants that thrive best in tropical or subtropical climates can grow in containers on balconies or sheltered patios in cooler climes and be brought indoors when the weather becomes cold.

CREATING YOUR LOVE GARDEN

Your love garden is an area that, as you tend it, will revive your own sense of self-love, especially if you are feeling lonely or unloved. Just a few different species or one or two love herbs or flowers can be enough to generate and maintain these powers.

Some love-aligned herbs and flowers may already be present in your well-being and prosperity gardens. If love is a major concern in your life right now, you might want to consider transplanting them or adding more of the same to a dedicated indoor or outdoor love garden. Here are some other suggestions for creating your love garden:

* If your love garden is outdoors, make a circular or heart-shaped flowerbed by marking its borders with stones or shells. It does not matter if this flowerbed encroaches on others in your garden or seeds or spores escape to form a wildflower area, as there can never be too much love.
* If your garden is indoors, create a circle of love flowers and herbs as potted plants circling a central love plant. Change the central plant regularly according to your current love priority.
* Empower or enchant your love garden as described in the well-being and prosperity garden sections, changing the words of your chants to focus on any specific love needs.
* Reenergize individual love plants whose qualities become important or, if love matters become a priority, the whole space.
* People trying to become pregnant later in life can become anxious if conception is not instant. This can actually hinder conception, both natural and IVF. As a remedy for anxiety, your floral garden may bring reassurance—don't discount a love flower garden if your primary motivation is love for a future child.

ROSE SPELL

Roses are a symbol of love in almost every culture and age, and each color has its own magical meaning. No love garden is complete without them. If you have only a confined space or live in a very cold climate, grow miniature roses indoors. Some people fill their love garden with all-purpose roses.

PINK: Attracting love · first love · new love · romance

RED: Lasting love and fidelity · fertility · increasing commitment in love · marriage or moving in together · passion

WHITE: Secret love · reconciliation

WILD ROSES: Secret admirer · vacation romance · long-distance love

YELLOW: Protection against jealousy and love rivals · love in the golden years or second or third time around

If you seek love, increased commitment, or rekindling of an ailing or past relationship, try this rose spell to draw a lover known or as yet unknown. If you pick a rose from your love garden to use, the spell power will be greatly enhanced.

You Will Need

- A green candle (color of Anael, archangel of love) or a rose-scented candle.
- A secure heatproof candle holder.
- A large fragrant rose with petals that are quite dry but not brown—use pink for love not yet found or at the friendship stage, red for putting impetus into a slow-moving or stagnant relationship and for marriage, or yellow if you have loved and lost and would like to love again
- Small barbecue tongs or sugar tongs
- A small ceramic or metal dish half filled with soil or sand to safely hold the burned petals
- A tall slender vase for the rose

Timing

Begin the spell at midnight on the night of the crescent moon for an unknown love or on any night up to the full moon for an existing friendship or relationship you would like to become more intense. The closer to the full moon, the more powerful the energies for increasing the pace of the relationship. You could use the waning moon for removing obstacles in the way of love.

The Spell

Place the candle in the holder. As you light the candle, say, *I call my love in fragrance and in fire. Far or near, known or hidden from my sight, so do I seek my love this night.*

Take a petal from the rose and, holding it carefully between your index finger and thumb or using the tongs for safety, carefully singe the corner of the petal in the candle flame until it browns.

As you burn the petal, say *I call my love in fragrance and in fire. Far or near, known or hidden from my sight, so do I seek my love this night. Burn rose, burn, that my love may for me yearn.*

Drop the burning petal into the dish, making sure the dish is not too near the candle. It does not matter if the petal burns completely or goes out.

Burn the second petal in the flame, saying the same words, and then drop the singed petal into the soil.

Burn the third and final petal and drop it into the dish, this time saying *Burn rose, burn, that my love may for me yearn. Flare and flame within us as desire. My love appears in candle fire.*

Hold the rose from which you have plucked the petals, and, looking into the candle flame, picture a misty figure moving toward you out of the light. Close your eyes and blink, and in the aura around the flame or in your mind's eye you may momentarily see a face, perhaps that of your present love.

If you are not in a relationship, the face may be of an unknown person yet to come into your life or someone you may have thought of as a friend or colleague but who could, if you wished, become much more.

If the misty figures are unclear, the time is not right for you to know the identity of your lover. Be patient, for the face may come to you in a dream. In the meantime, continue to tend the rosebush from which you took the rose, knowing that love will come at the time and in the place that is right.

If you are in a relationship and you see just mists, it is not a bad omen, but rather reflecting uncertainties you have not voiced even to yourself or a need for greater communication on one or both sides.

Blow out the candle, sending the light to your present or future love or to call back a former partner. Put the rose in a vase of water, keep it until the petals fade, and then scatter them to the winds. Bury the burned petals in the soil, if possible, beneath your rosebush or miniature indoor rose.

CRYSTALS IN YOUR LOVE GARDEN

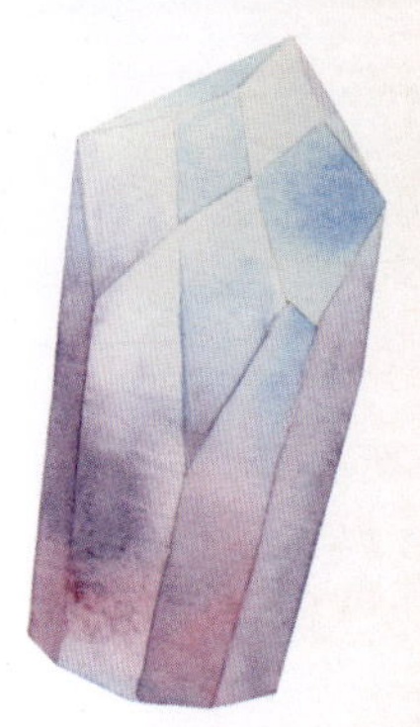

Crystals buried in a love garden area or in individual plant pots can greatly increase the flow of love energies.

AMETHYST: Reconciliation and harmony if there have been quarrels or separation, disruption, or intrusion by others in your love or family life

GREEN AVENTURINE: Good fortune if you have been unlucky in love • fertility • self-love should you doubt your ability to attract the right love

GREEN JADE: Committed love and fidelity • a twin soul • love in the golden years

PINK ROSE QUARTZ: Gentle flow of new or young love • restoration of trust after betrayal • love of family, friends, pets • most importantly, self-love

RED GARNET: Passion • protection against partners or relatives who are emotional vampires and against possessiveness

Plant a crystal in the compass points (approximate is fine) of your love flower and herb area plus one in the center: aventurine in the north, amethyst in the east, red garnet in the south, and rose quartz in the west, with jade in the center—or whatever feels right to you.

LOVE MAGIC WITH FLOWERS AND HERBS

Flowers and fragrant herbs can be used as the whole growing flower in situ or placed in a vase, as fresh or dried petals or flowerheads, as potpourri, and in oils and incenses. The growing fragrant garden offers concentrated energies and immediate and ongoing uplifting of our clairsentient and claircognizant (sixth sense) gifts. It fills our aura energy field with radiance, not least as a boost to self-esteem if love is absent from your life.

Including one or two of your own love garden flowers or herbs in any magical workings or meditation strengthens the powerful connection with the love you are growing.

Empowered charm bags (see page 102) of fragrant dried petals can be carried or worn near the heart to attract love or a particular lover.

Teas made of chamomile, jasmine, lavender, rose, or rose hip can be offered to a lover or would-be lover and stirred—silently, add your wish or empowerment—for the connection to grow. This practice is also an effective method of encouraging embryonic office romances.

Fragrant baths are another wonderful way to enhance love energies. You may use commercially prepared blends or make your own at home by placing herbs and flowers into a porous sachet and then adding it to bathwater before a special date, lovemaking, or going out socially where you hope to meet love. Baths of this sort are natural aphrodisiacs and open your aura energy field to call love and increase charisma.

When doing love rituals, use fresh petals plucked from a flower, or buy or make potpourri containing love flowers and herbs. If creating a magic circle while casting love spells, use herbs and flowers to act as the Earth element in lieu of salt.

Herbal teabags, if split open, offer a whole range of herbs and flowers used in love magic, as will the cooking section of your local grocery store. Empower herbs in a love spell and afterward use them in cooking a meal for your lover.

Make love poppets, featureless dolls filled with dried love herbs and plants—again, where possible, including some from your garden—and set them side by side in a basket of fragrant petals or gently tied with ribbons in three loose knots, saying, *Three times the lover's knot secures, willingly may this love endure*. Hang the ribbons, joined at the top with a single knot, behind the bedroom door. Keep the dolls face to face near the bed before lovemaking.

Love Plants

Having used some of the following plants elsewhere in this book, I will now focus on their specific love-attracting powers. Many are multipurpose, so you may find collecting or growing certain core plants will enable you to explore a multitude of magical uses.

BASIL: Passion • committed love • fidelity, especially if one of the lovers is frequently absent • protection against those who would divide a loving couple

CAMELLIA: Pink, in many shades, signifying gentle love without limits or conditions or a beloved absent lover • white for young, first, or unconsummated love • red for romance and passion • all camellias for family loyalty at home or within a family business • given in an enchanted bouquet on love anniversaries and Valentine's Day to bring everlasting unity in love

CARNATION: Red for passion, calling back absent or past love, or overcoming betrayal • pink for expressing gratitude for a living mother's love (also sometimes red), friendship, increasing group or team bonding • white for maternal love lost, remembering those mothers who have passed over or are not in our lives, love in later years, truth in love

Camellia

CHAMOMILE: Affection • gentle love • increases self-love, especially after abuse • restoring confidence after betrayal • fertility • family love and reconciliation in love

CHRYSANTHEMUM: Red for passion, marriage, and motherhood • yellow for ending relationships with kindness • white for truth and love forever

GARDENIA: For all moon love spells, especially on the full moon • attracting love and romance • spiritual love • left on the doorstep indicates a secret admirer • secret love • for a loving household, especially multigenerational

GERANIUM: Fertility • friendship • the growth of love • protection against jealousy and love rivals • bringing or restoring harmony to the home • healing coldness and indifference • diminishing the effect of emotional blackmail in relationships and guilt trips

Chamomile

HIBISCUS: Sensuality, charisma, and radiance • love and passion, especially later in life • worn in Hawaii and Tahiti behind the left ear to indicate a woman is in a relationship, but on the right side to indicate she is ready to find love

JASMINE: Attracting love and increasing passion • secret love • making dreams come true • discovering the identity of a secret admirer • enhancing male potency and female fertility • night and moon love rituals • protection against emotional vampires and love rivals • increasing self-love and personal radiance • melting emotional blockages and fears

KNOTWEED: All binding spells against those who would damage a relationship through jealousy • encouraging loyalty in lovers or friends • keeping promises in love • bringing partners' existing children into a united family

LAVENDER: A major love flower and herb • like roses, can be substituted for any other flower • kindness in love and friendship • mending quarrels • banishing guilt • protection against abuse of all kinds • attracting new love and romance • restoring trust • encouraging lasting faithful love • family happiness • healing quarrels and sorrow

LEMON BALM (MELISSA): In love sachets and added to wine to call love or a specific lover into your life • fertility • letting go of emotional ties and healing wounds of betrayal • ending love gently

Jasmine

Mint

LEMON VERBENA: Purification of bad atmospheres after love quarrels • protection against hexes or ill-wishes on a love relationship by jealous relatives or rivals • maintaining love and friendship through the years and life changes • increasing family happiness

MEADOWSWEET: Lasting love • reconciliation • diminishing rivalry in love • increasing peace both within the self and among family members • increasing unity within the community and the wider world

MIMOSA: Attracting a wealthy lover • love later in life • overcoming grief for loved ones who have died or left forever • sustaining love in bad times • also for maintaining and restoring connection with absent lovers • keeping secrets • secret trysts

MINT: Increasing sexual desire • healing sorrows in love • banishing those who would harm a love relationship or family happiness, especially former partners • romantic vacations and getaways • seeing through false lovers

MOONWORT: Love rituals associated with the phases of the moon • romance and attracting love on the waxing moon • passion and fertility on the full moon • ending destructive relationships and co-dependency on the waning moon

ROSEMARY: Bringing lovers together after an absence or estrangement • increasing passion • recalling and reviving old love • reconciliation with estranged family, friends, or love • renewal of vows

VALERIAN: Love and love divination • dreams of a lover known or unknown • hope when relationships hit a bad period • reuniting those parted by anger or circumstance

VERVAIN: Love that transforms enemies into friends or indifference into passion • aphrodisiac traditionally given in a bouquet for the honeymoon

VIOLET: Restoring trust • keeping secrets and secret love • sugar violets or infusions with sugar for romance with an undemonstrative partner

In the next chapter, we look at how plants can be used to look into the future.

Rosemary

3

ENCHANTED PLANTS

PLANTS HAVE a long history when it comes to their place in ritual, spellwork, and divination. For centuries, ordinary people and village wise men and women used plants to look into the future and to connect with nature spirits and their own inner psyche. In the modern world, children and young lovers still pluck daisy petals asking yes/no questions, such as *he loves me, he loves me not*, until all the petals have been picked and the answer received.

Rods made from hazel are used by modern dowsers just like traditional dowsers of years past to detect where subterranean water, lost items, or earth energies lie.

In this chapter, I will describe two of my favorite methods of plant divination, which are both easy and yet startlingly accurate: herb scrying, or floating dried herbs on water to create images to ask questions, and flower psychometry to help self and others to obtain psychic answers to questions where information is confusing or not accessible to the conscious mind.

Herb Scrying

Scrying by floating herbs on the surface of a bowl of water to create images from the herb formations to answer questions is an ancient form of divination. This was practiced widely in many countries because herbs were available to ordinary people in hedgerows and gardens. Crystal spheres and tarot cards were until recent times the province of the wealthy, and tea leaves and coffee grounds were beyond the purses of common folk until the late 1800s.

Even then, divination remained the province of the family matriarch or, for serious matters, the village wise woman. Herb scrying is a very personal and user-friendly method of obtaining answers to questions that elude us or whose answers are just over the horizon. It is an excellent prelude to seeing more static crystal sphere images, as the herb images on the surface of the water are three-dimensional and moving.

HOW TO SCRY WITH HERBS

To try this technique, first you must gather your herbs. Here are twelve that are especially good for the practice, but in theory you can use any nontoxic herb. The dried versions you buy in grocery stores are best. Culinary herbs are generally safe to handle. Choose broad-leafed, not powdery, herbs, to make distinct images. Some scryers will match the herbs to the nature of the question, but this is not necessary. You can use any of the herbs for any question and mix different herbs. A brief meaning is given here for each.

BASIL: Money • protection

CHIVES: Bad habits • change

CHAMOMILE: Children • reconciliation

DILL: Neutralizing envy • the home

FENNEL: Relocation • travel

LAVENDER HEADS (DRIED): Love • healing

MARJORAM: Removing neighborhood hostility • marriage

PARSLEY: Luck • passion • one of the four traditional divinatory herbs

ROSEMARY: Absent love • memory • one of the four traditional divinatory herbs

SAGE: Employment • examinations • one of the four traditional divinatory herbs

TARRAGON: Countering bullying • persistence

THYME: Preventing or neutralizing curses • good health and long life • one of the four traditional divinatory herbs

Aside from the herbs themselves, you will need a large glass or ceramic white bowl half-filled with water. If working with a group on a joint question, you can use a basin, as long as there is plenty of light, whether natural light or candlelight, to shine on the surface of the water.

Slowly add the herbs you are using to the bowl, a few at a time.

Either swirl the bowl several times alternately clockwise and counterclockwise, or stir the water in both directions with the index finger of the hand with which you write or clockwise using a clear crystal point.

Enchant and empower the herbs by softly and continuously reciting the purpose of the divination until you sense or see in your mind a green mist over the bowl.

Herbs floating on the surface of the water create moving physical images that can be interpreted by your psychic senses. Images will resemble the stick figures children draw—children, in fact, are invariably brilliant at herb scrying. You will mainly identify separate images, but some may join and change rapidly, and occasionally you may see a whole scene. If so, identify yourself and significant others within it. Turn the bowl around in your hands or on the table as often as you like to study the images from all angles.

Practice recognizing images before asking actual questions to become more proficient at identifying different images as they appear without assigning any meanings. Work fast before your logical mind intrudes.

If you aren't seeing any recognizable shapes in the water, close your eyes, open them, blink, and stare at one herb formation and say out loud what the image is without consciously identifying it. This will unblock your psyche. Do this for all of them and you will find connections.

To obtain answers, first ask a question that is currently of importance to you. Note any images that instantly appear. Keep naming the images rapidly one after the other, so your logical mind does not intrude. It may help to record the session on your phone or take a photo of any particularly clear image so you don't forget any. You may become aware that one image is larger and clearer than the others and appears almost immediately. This is often the heart of the answer, and the other images will add information to this central theme.

Flower Psychometry

Flowers and flowering herbs are powerful transmitters of the life force and can provide a clear psychic link between the person who owns or chooses a flower and the diviner. The flower acts as the channel, and as with any form of divination, messages will come from the angels, guides, and, in the case of flowers and flowering herbs, from devas or nature angels, wise ancestors, and the nature essence some believe live in every flower.

Psychometry means psychic touch, whereby through your fingertips you acquire impressions psychically in images, words, and feelings that can provide you with insight into the potentials of yourself or a third party transmitting their energies through the flower of what they most need to know.

FLOWER ANGELS

GURID: A midsummer angel whose halo is made of all summer flowers. Gurid will advise how to bring more happiness and fun into your life.

JOPHIEL: Angel of paradise on earth, with a halo of flowers and berries. Ask this angel how you can attain fulfillment as well as success.

SACHLUPH: Angel of flowers and herbs with wings of white petals. Ask Sachluph to bring more beauty into your life.

WHY FLOWER PSYCHOMETRY?

Flowers and flowering herbs are traditionally a good focus for personal psychometry or psychic touch as even cut flowers are filled with the life force that absorbs psychic impressions from the person who has chosen the flower—not just immediate issues, but their core self.

The flower links past, present, and future. For those who find psychic exploration challenging, flower psychometry automatically and spontaneously amplifies psychic connection, and as a result previously dormant powers will be activated afterward in other psychic arts, especially psychometry.

USING FLOWERS AS A PERSONAL MEDIUM

You can practice flower psychometry alone, using a favorite flower growing in the garden, in a pot, or purchased from a florist or garden center that attracts you. Start by using fragrant flowers, as the scent will awaken your psychic clairsentience and make connection with your psyche, as well as the essences of nature spirits or devas and angels. Initially, you can either work with a single flower or focus on a bed of growing flowers outside, where you may connect more easily with higher spirits and angels.

If you wish, ask a specific question, or you can allow the messages you need to hear to emerge in your inner voice via the flowers. Look at the flowers until you have a desire to close your eyes. Then close your eyes to allow the color of the flower to fill your senses, and gradually picture the flower to fill your mind using your clairvoyant vision.

When you are ready open your eyes, blink and allow words to flow into your mind (see color meanings on pages 94–95). Record the messages you receive from your flowers, as it is too easy to forget as life intrudes.

Inhale any fragrance, slowly breathing in the scent and allowing any darkness or stagnation to flow out in a gentle rhythm by inhaling through the nose and exhaling in a sigh through the mouth, or using any breathing method that feels right—or just let it happen.

Next, gently move your hands upward over a chosen flower's stem, leaves, and then the flower itself, or the pot or vase if you know the flower irritates your skin if held for a prolonged period. You may become aware of the nature essence within the flower. Move your hands softly, or trace spirals in the air with a single finger, from the center to the outermost petals. Allow words, sounds, impressions, and feelings to flow between you and the plant. These may answer a question or give you a sense of healing and well-being.

Thank the essence of the plant, slowly withdraw your hands, and sit quietly, thanking the plant for its wisdom. Give it special care and, if necessary, wash your hands if you experience skin irritation from flowers. For some people, looking at the flower and allowing it to fill your mind may be sufficient to trigger messages. This is known as remote psychometry.

FLOWER COLORS

These can be predictive or refer to present situations and feelings, depending on what the psychometrist feels.

RED: Scarlet: passion and ambition fulfilled through action • pale red: feeling intimidated • dull red: suppressed resentment

ORANGE: Desires needing to be expressed, especially for independence • fertility • pale orange: loss of identity • dark orange: need for privacy • bright orange: confidence

YELLOW: Joy and openness • confidence • travel prospects • lemon yellow: the need for logic • mustard yellow: suppressed jealousy

GREEN: Greenery and rich green flowers: happiness in love, maybe still being pursued, messages from nature spirits • dark green: love in later years, fidelity • dull green: possessiveness

BLUE: Pale blue: altruism and idealism • rich or bright blue: wisdom, career success, creativity, desire for justice • dark blue: overconcern with convention

PURPLE: Spiritual connections • messages from ancestors • revelation of secrets • pale purple: unworldly, secret love

WHITE: High spiritual ideals • messages from angels and guides • leadership • lofty ambitions

PINK: Bright pink: lover • matters concerning pregnancy, children, and animals • practicality • pale pink: gentle and reconciliatory

BROWN: Rich bronze: property matters, practical concerns • acquiring money • what is lasting

GOLD: Success in the way most desired • wealth • greatness • fame • fortune

More than one color in a flower indicates versatility but also changeability. Look at the shades and colors nearest the center for the true nature.

FLOWER STRUCTURE

The physical structure of the flower can also provide information during psychometry.

STALK/STEM: The stem of the flower is often seen as a symbolic representation of a person's life journey. Starting from the bottom of the stem, each point upward brings you nearer to the present moment. As you move along, you may intuitively sense how many years are represented along this path. The future is revealed where the stem meets the flower itself, offering insight into what lies ahead.

LEAVES: Leaves reflect helpful outer circumstances, influential people in your life right now, or external hazards according to what you feel. Discolored or torn leaves indicate the need to take greater care of yourself. Many leaves suggest a lot of responsibilities but also support.

FLOWERS: If buds are present, it suggests plans not yet achieved or not initiated. A single flower suggests going it alone by choice or necessity. A double flower suggests a twin soul. Smaller flowers indicate fertility (if children are desired) or existing child-related matters. If the flower stands apart from the leaves, it means travel or an independent venture may be imminent. If immersed in leaves or other flowers, collective ventures are the way forward unless one flower is being crushed. Flowers represent what you are manifesting. An opening flower alerts you to be ready to act. A flower in full bloom says you are on the right track. Visible seeds represent the chance of gain in the way most desired. A fading or closing flower points to the ending of a phase. The inner flower or stamens represent the inner you. Any berries or fruit indicate money coming, but if withered, it means an opportunity missed.

Safe Flowers for Psychometry

If you are asking people to a psychometry event where you or they read one another's flowers, you may be worried that you will be given a toxic flower or offer one to which someone is allergic. However, there are several easy precautions that can be taken, including washing your hands immediately after handling a flower, if you are worried.

If you are drawn to a flower you fear may be hazardous to you or that you are allergic to, wear thin surgical gloves (not the thicker kitchen kind) while handling the plant. The gloves will allow the delicate chakra energy that centers in your palms to flow, and your fingers will still be sensitive, just as a surgeon is able to carry out intricate nerve surgery when wearing gloves.

In fact, you do not even need to touch the flower to gain psychic information. The flower will have picked up spiritual energies from the aura of the person owning the flower, and you yourself have an invisible psychic aura that extends all around you. You can lay the flower flat on a table and pass your hands or just the index finger of your writing hand a centimeter or two above and all around the flower, and you will feel its aura energy field as a tingling as it meets your energy. This form of remote psychometry is successfully used in museums where artifacts are in glass cases; you can pick up the energies just by holding your palms close to the case.

FLOWERS ESPECIALLY SUITABLE FOR FLOWER PSYCHOMETRY

All listed here should be nontoxic for most adults, but check with an authoritative source to see if they are safe for children.

AFRICAN DAISY: Red, yellow, pink, purple, white • joy • celebrations of all kinds • transformations • makeovers

ALYSSUM: Small and often in groups among leaves • white, dark pink, purple • illusion and deception • overcoming anger and destructive people

AMARANTH: Red, purple, fuchsia, burgundy • grief and loss • fertility • overcoming heartache in love • new beginnings

ASTILBE: Feathery flowers • red, pink, lavender, dark purple, white, reds • passion • influential people • pink: maternal issues • white: first love or love after loss • purple: spiritual gifts

BOUGAINVILLEA: Purple, mauve, pink, apricot, red, yellow • self-esteem • socializing • self-image • new careers • businesses

BROMELIAD: Multicolored leaves in red, green, orange, purple, yellow • flowering central blossoms in red, blue, pink, yellow, purple • money • business affairs • security

CAMELLIA: Red, pink, white, yellow • family loyalty • family businesses • money • acquisition of wealth • handle with care if you have sensitive skin

CARNATION: Pink, white, red, peach, yellow, green (green is popular among those of Celtic origin on St Patrick's Day) • mothering • maternal loss • absent mothers • past loves • past lives

DAHLIA: Red, yellow, pink, orange, white • travel • celebrations • letting go of the past • overcoming fears

FORSYTHIA: Yellow • long-term dreams and desires • joy after sorrow • any slow-moving or long-term projects

FREESIA: White, yellow, orange, blue • clarity where there is confusion • understanding • overcoming blockages in the way of desired change

FUCHSIA: Red and purple combined • love matters • unique abilities • family • overcoming betrayal and resisting temptation

GARDENIA: White • connecting with the spirit of the plant • love matters • house moves

GERANIUM: Pink, red, purple, bronze, white • worries about domestic conflict or trouble in the workplace

HYACINTH: Blue, white, pink, lilac • self-esteem issues and rebuilding trust after betrayal • new beginnings • opposition in love • toxic if bulbs are eaten • can cause skin irritation if the bulbs are handled

JACOB'S LADDER: White, pastel blue, purplish-blue, purple, white • spiritual and psychic development • messages from angels, guides, ancestors, and plant devas

Forsythia

JASMINE: Also known as queen of the night or fae bells • white, pink, yellow • love • sexual problems • fertility • moon mysteries • connection with nature spirits

LAVENDER: White, pink, blue, all shades of purple • healing • new and young love • self-love • financial affairs • escaping abuse • teenagers

LILAC: Blue, deep purple, pale violet • home and family • absent friends, lovers, and relatives • past lives

MARIGOLD: Golden orange • the law and officialdom • unrequited love • messages from nature spirits • if you have sensitive skin, be careful touching the sap

PANSY: Blue, orange, pink, white, red, purple, mauve, lavender, bronze, white, multicolored • families • love returning, maybe after years • thoughts of home • fidelity

PASSIONFLOWER: Pink and white or yellow and purple • revealing strong positive feelings • twin souls • love under difficulty

PETUNIA: Pink, purple, white, yellow, green, blue, multicolored • vacations, • creativity • environmental concerns • settling into committed relationships

PHLOX: Pink • unity among partners, family, friends, and colleagues • contemplating marriage, major love commitment, or a proposal

ROSE: Pink, lavender, plum-purple, burgundy, orange, red, yellow, green • love • reconciliation • fertility • money • babies and children • adolescent girls

SNAPDRAGON: Blue, pink, white • injustice • hostility from others • identifying deceit

TUBEROSE: Waxy flowers that bloom at night • white • love • reconciliation • messages from ancestors • receiving news, especially from overseas • sexual matters • mildly toxic if ingested, handle with care

VIOLET: Various shades of purple • loyalty • self-consciousness • denying gifts • uncovering secrets • untrustworthiness

ZINNIA: Red, orange, deep pink, yellow, green, often with deep yellow center • connection with indigenous wise men and women • acclaim for achievements • friendship • not toxic, but some people have a skin reaction to the sap

DIVINATORY CARDS

You can also make a divinatory card set of your favorite herbs and flowers, as many or few as you wish, printed or drawn on pieces of card, each with a blank side. Write beneath each a basic meaning found in this book, for example, *Cinnamon* for *swift powerful action,* or *Fennel* for *travel*. Make the description on the card as detailed as you wish. Shuffle the pack as you ask a question and pick three facedown cards for an answer.

Spell Bags, Wish Jars, Amulets, Charm Bags

Empowered spell or charm bags draw together different herbs with similar energies or combine different herbal energies for a specific purpose—for example, to protect the home against natural disasters and paranormal and human attack, to attract the right love, and to change misfortune to good luck. As the bag is carried, worn, or kept in the home or the workplace, the empowered herbs continue to endow the user or the place in which they're kept with their energies.

In practice, the terms *amulet*, *talisman*, *charm bag*, and *spell bag* can be used interchangeably, although in theory amulets tend to refer to protective purposes and talismans to an herbal bag created for a specific purpose for a defined period of time. Herbal charms are more open-ended and can be used to attract ongoing, specific results, such as good fortune, growing prosperity, or health. The term *spell bag* rather than *charm bag* can be used when a full spell is used to empower the bag.

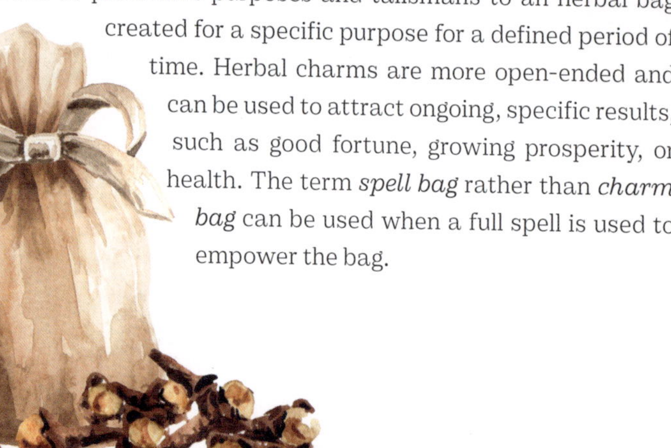

SPELL BAGS

You can spend a small fortune buying a spell bag from a New Age store, but creating your own is easy and more powerful. It's as simple as filling a vessel with your intentions and energies along with ingredients procured from your spice rack or pantry. Here are some tips for getting started.

Since every herb has a magical meaning, by combining different herbs in different proportions, spell bags (the term I will mainly use) can focus on specific wishes or powers. You activate the power of your spell bag with the purpose and target of the bag—which should always be positive even if protective—as well as the time frame over which the spell should work, during the mixing process, whether a single herb or mix.

Make a spell bag on any of the three or four days before the full moon after dusk to attract good things, on any of the three days after the full moon for protection, or on the night of the full moon for major purposes, change, urgent needs, or conceiving a child.

ASSEMBLING YOUR SPELL BAG

Most people use either a drawstring bag or a fabric purse to hold their empowered herbs. Most spell bags are pocket-sized or tiny enough to be hung around the neck or pinned to undergarments. For a household protection spell bag, you could make one the size of a small evening bag to hide or hang over an entrance where air circulates.

USING YOUR SPELL BAG

Add your chosen herbs one at a time to a ceramic bowl, naming the purpose of each as you add it. Mix with a wooden spoon if you wish, naming all of them in a slow chant as you mix, plus any time frame. Alternatively, add them separately straight into the bag, in the right proportions. Close or tie the bag with three, six, or nine knots and set it in the center of the table of your special natural place.

Now take a lighted incense stick in each hand, and, using them like smoke pens, write the purpose of the spell bag with the incense in your dominant hand all around the spell bag, and the name of the person and the time scale, if there is one, plus a secret message of power.

Then, hovering in the air a few centimeters over the bag, hold the incense stick in your dominant hand and make smoke spirals, moving clockwise. Switch hands, holding the incense in your non-dominant hand, then spiral counterclockwise. While making smoke spirals, continuously recite a simple rhythmic empowerment or protection chant, such as *Bring success and prosperity, if it is right to be, before the moon is past, so this wish I cast.* With spell bags, even if they're for protection and healing, you'll need to build up the power to get them moving.

When you can chant and move the incense sticks no faster, join the sticks for a second, saying, *Flame and flare as I count three, the power of this bag I take in me.* Plunge the incense sticks into a dish of soil.

GETTING THE MIX RIGHT

Generally, magic or spell bags contain three, five, seven, or nine different items. Enclose nuts or seeds in a knot of cloth within the bag to make them one item for growth, fertility, prosperity, and gradual improvement in any area of life. The number may itself be significant.

For example, the tearlike seeds called Job's tears offer protection against any sorrow and are said to absorb pain or sickness. Three seeds in a bag bring good luck; five bring rapid growth of what is desired, such as love or money; and seven will grant wishes made when the bag is sealed. You can use juniper berries or small nuts or cloves in the same way.

As well as herbs, add spices, dried flower petals or heads, or dried tree leaves chopped or ground very small (an old coffee bean grinder is a good tool to have). The proportions of each ingredient will depend on the emphasis of the powers you want in the mix.

For example, for a love herbal bag, you might mix rose or lavender for romance, and then add a few dried bay leaves (the cooking kind) for faithfulness, a sprinkling of cinnamon or ginger for passion, and finally yarrow or sage for a lasting relationship. You can vary the proportions and mix and match exactly the right blend.

Herb bags are said to be active until the fragrance fades, when they can be replaced if needed for ongoing protection or power. The eve of the Summer Solstice (around June 20) or Midsummer Eve (June 23) are often when spell bags are replaced and left from dawn to noon the following day.

When they are inactive or no longer needed, herbs should be scattered in the air if used for attracting purposes or buried if the bag was created for banishing or binding purposes.

A collective spell bag made by a psychometry group for an individual or collective needs can have thirteen items or one item for each member of a group.

WISH JARS

These are a more recent addition to the magical world, usually made in clear wide-necked jars with sealable lids. They are slow-acting: Their power builds up over weeks or months. They have the added benefit of strengthening your own initiative and determination as the powers call toward you the manifestation of the desire or need incubating within the jar.

To create a wish jar, first define what you wish to incubate. Then collect what you will need.

- A strip of paper
- A blue pen
- Scissors (optional)
- One jar with a sealable lid; it need not be large
- A few of your favorite crystals
- A supply of three or four dried herbs and petals, at least one of which should be fragrant and the others related to the need, such as basil for money or courage, chamomile for family

matters, and calendula (marigold) for legal concerns; mix and match to bring together different aspects of what you are calling

Write the wish and the desired time frame on the strip of paper with the pen, reciting it aloud as you write it. Then tear or cut the wish into pieces and set it at the bottom of the jar with a few of your favorite crystals. Next, add layers of the herbs and flowers, making sure the ingredients are dry or dried. The jar need not be more than half full. Whisper the wish into the jar and put the lid on it.

Keep the jar in a sunny place. Every day, first thing in the morning, hold your jar, whisper the wish, shake it nine times without taking off the lid, and return it to its place.

Use the jar until the contents fade, or when the wish is granted, and then spread the contents to the winds.

HERBS TO USE

The following are suggested herbs that can be used in amulets, talismans, charm bags and spell bags and wish jars. You are sure to have some on your cooking shelf or at your local health food/

remedy store. Make sure ingredients are dry to prevent mold from forming in the bag.

Check online for other uses of your chosen herbs and the best herb forms to use, whether powdered, dried flowers or roots, and also for contraindications such as pregnancy. When you are making these magical containers you will not be ingesting the herbs, though you may want to avoid inhaling them if you have allergies. Some herbs are best avoided to touch, if pregnant or breast-feeding. And see the note on page 97 about wearing surgical gloves to protect from possible allergic reactions.

Choose from the list below up to three or four herbs that represent what you most wish for or need (a single one if you prefer). Experiment mixing and matching, remembering to have at least one fragrant herb in any mix.

ADAM AND EVE ROOT: Love • marriage proposals • fidelity

AGRIMONY: Protection • peaceful sleep • returning negativity to sender

ALLSPICE: Money • luck • healing • passion • fertility

ALMOND/ALMOND BLOSSOM: Abundance • prosperity • fertility • love without limits

ALOE, BITTER: Preventing gossip and false friends

ANGELICA (ARCHANGEL ROOT): Protection of the home • speculation • bringing angelic influences into your life

ANISE: Reducing fears of attack and anxiety about aging and infirmity

APPLE/APPLE BLOSSOM: Fertility • good fortune • abundance • health • love • long life

ARBUTUS, STRAWBERRY TREE: Protection of the young • exorcism

ARNICA: Midsummer • harvest • sun healing rituals (especially of abuse and neglect)

Bergamot

BASIL: Love • protection against intruders, accidents, and attack • wealth • fertility • conquering fear of flying

BAY LAUREL LEAF: Psychic powers • strength • marriage • fertility • fidelity • prosperity

BERGAMOT (CITRUS AND WILD): Successful property deals and investments • reducing addictions, fears, and destructive relationships

BLACK SNAKEROOT (BLACK COHOSH): Bringing courage • male potency • passion

BLEEDING HEART (LOCKS AND KEYS): Overcoming a betrayal or loss in love • moving on

BLOODLEAF: Stopping gossip • removing spiteful people from your life

BLOODROOT: Reconciliation within the family • overcoming sibling and stepfamily/ex-partner rivalries

BLUE COHOSH: Restoring natural cycles and harmony to stressed modern lives (especially for mature women) • fertility • protection against spite

BUCKWHEAT SEEDS: Keeping away poverty, debt, and all malevolent influences

BUTTERBUR: Fertility • good fortune • health • love • protection • the root or dried leaves in a brown amulet bag set above the front door protect from all danger

CAPERS: Courage to stand against bullying • protection against the evil eye of jealousy and envy

CAPSICUM: Determination • power

CARAWAY SEEDS: Protection of property against theft or damage • improving mental powers

CAT'S CLAW: Defense against spite and jealousy • protection of pets

CATNIP (CATMINT): Cat magic • animal healing • love • beauty • happiness in home

CAT'S-EAR (FALSE DANDELION): Cat-healing amulets and spells • becoming psychically aware of gossip and rumors behind your back

CELERY SEEDS: Potency • money • protection • bringing travel

Red Clover

CHAMOMILE: Gentle love • self-love (especially after abuse) • lessening addictions

CHIA SEEDS: Preventing gossip, false friends, and deception

CLOVER, RED AND WHITE: Protection • banishing negativity • success • good luck • employment

CLOVES: Protection • banishing negativity • love • having owed money returned

COLTSFOOT: Love • visions • peace • tranquility • protection of horses

COMFREY: Protection of travelers, documents, arrangements, and luggage

COMMON RUE: Protection • purification, wards off negative influences and dispels evil spirits • good fortune

CUMIN SEEDS: Protection (especially of homes, property, and cars)

DEERTONGUE: Calling a gentle, loving partner (especially in LGBTQ relationships)

DEVIL'S CLUB: Removing spiritual blockages • repelling curses and ill-wishes

DEVIL'S SHOESTRING: Protection • gambling • good luck • power • employment

DILL: Keeping home, loved ones, and land safe

ELDERBERRIES/ELDERFLOWERS: Increasing clairvoyance • nature spirit magic

EUCALYPTUS: Moving long-standing official and legal problems or neighborhood disputes toward resolution

EYEBRIGHT: Increasing clairvoyance • awareness of what is hidden or untrue

FENNEL: Travel • holidays • relocation • journeys of all kinds • protection of animals and small children

FENUGREEK: Prosperity • health • strength • protection against theft (especially online)

FIGWORT (KNOTTED FIGWORT): Protection against the evil eye; health for the user

FIREWEED (ROSEBAY WILLOWHERB): Rituals for the fall • rebirth • bringing life to stagnant situations

FLEABANE: Removing malevolent spirits from the home • resisting unwanted sexual pressures

GALANGAL (LOW JOHN THE CONQUEROR ROOT): Justice • success in all official matters

GARLIC: Health • psychic protection (especially against unfriendly spirits)

GINGER: Energy • health • bringing or renewing passion • money-making enterprises • any matter needing speed

HIGH JOHN THE CONQUEROR ROOT (*IPOMOEA PURGA*): Money • success • luck • protection against psychic attack or ill-wishers

HONEYSUCKLE: Sweetening overly critical people

HOPS: Healing • peaceful sleep • money • recovery from loss or debt

HOUNDSTONGUE: Preventing problems with other people's dogs • preventing lies against you being believed

IMPATIENS (JEWELWEED, TOUCH-ME-NOT): Keeping away stalkers, intruders, and those who interfere as well as paranormal attack

IVY: Marriage • fidelity • committed relationships • overcoming emotional blackmail • restoring lost love

JASMINE: Attracting love • increasing passion • secret love • making dreams come true • enhancing male potency

JOB'S TEARS SEEDS: Good luck • wishes granted

JUNIPER BERRIES: Increasing male potency • new beginnings • money • luck • purifying homes

LAVENDER: Healing • protection (especially of children) • health • friendship • romance

LEMON: Night magic • purification • removing addictions and destructive ties from the past

LEMON BALM (MELISSA): Increasing abundance and all good things in your life; reversing bad luck • granting wishes

Juniper

LEMONGRASS: Repelling spite • protection against jealousy, the evil eye, thieves, and bad neighbors • moves of all kinds • removing what is redundant in your life

LEMON MINT: Concentration • focus • avoiding and clearing misunderstandings

LEMON VERBENA: Purification • maintaining love and friendship • preventing interference by others into love relationships

LOTUS ROOT: New opportunities • blessings in whatever area they are sought • ability to open any doors to career or business

LUCKY HAND ROOT: Employment • luck • protection • money • safe travel • gambling

MARJORAM, SWEET: Driving away loneliness and fears of abandonment

MEADOW RUE: Mothers • Goddess charms • thawing of coldness in relationships

MEADOWSWEET: Lasting love • happiness • reconciliation • family and global peace

MINT: Purification • love • healing • increasing psychic powers • protection during travel

MONKEY-LADDER PODS: Banishing all negative wishing and earthly and paranormal mind manipulation

MOONWORT: Money • love • harmony • healing

MUGWORT: Psychic powers • prophetic dreams • protection on journeys from predators (human and otherwise)

ORANGE: Marriage • love commitment • fertility • health • passion • developing creative talents • fame • fortune

PARROT'S BEAK: Bringing calm • ability to connect with other dimensions • preventing or treating addiction

PARSLEY: Passion • physical, emotional, and psychic protection • prevention of bullying • divination

PASSIONFLOWER: Finding a twin soul • love forever • reuniting of lovers separated by distance

PATCHOULI: Earth energies • attracting moneymaking opportunities

PENNYROYAL: Strength • protection • peace • banishing debt

PIPSISSEWA (SPOTTED WINTERGREEN): Attracting good spirits and your own spirit guides • a money magnet

POKE ROOT: Breaking curses and hexes • courage • deterring hostile neighbors

POT MARIGOLD (*CALENDULA OFFICINALIS*): Legal matters • protection • prophetic dreams • growing love

PURSLANE, COMMON OR GOLDEN: Restful sleep • protection against attack in potentially dangerous situations

RAGWEED: Driving away fears (both real and internal) • healing the planet

RAGWORT: Protection • increasing libido in women • believed in medieval times to be used as brooms by witches to fly / astrally project

RATTLESNAKE ROOT: Protection from false friends • money • competitions • speculation

ROSE: Romance • love • fidelity • healing babies, children, animals, older people, and all who have been abused

SAGE: Long life • health • wisdom • protection • justice • house renovations and moves

SAW PALMETTO: Strengthening male potency and reproductive system

SCORPION WEED: Allaying fears of spiteful family members or work colleagues so you can deal decisively

SEAWEED (INCLUDING BLADDERWRACK AND KELP): Safe travel by sea and overseas • action after stagnation

SELF-HEAL OR WOUNDWORT: Healing inner and outer wounds and secret sorrows

SKULLCAP: Business partnerships • investment • attracting gifts and resources • love • fidelity • peace

SOUTHERN JOHN ROOT (DIXIE JOHN ROOT): Marriage proposals • passion • making you irresistible to a lover

SUMBUL: Good luck • gambling • speculation • lottery tickets

TARRAGON: Associated with dragons and serpent goddesses • courage • new beginnings • regeneration • new targets

TORMENTIL: Protection when practicing mediumship • lasting faithful love • keeping evil entities from the home

UNICORN ROOT, FALSE: Male potency • fertility • pregnancy • preventing trickery and scams

UNICORN ROOT, TRUE: Astral projection • connection with magical animals • protection of young girls

VALERIAN: Love • quiet sleep • protection against outer hostility and inner fears • reuniting those parted by anger

VANILLA: Love • fidelity • marriage vows • renewal of vows • money • well-being • health • harmony

VERVAIN: Transforming enemies into friends • peaceful sleep • healing • protection of the home

VETIVER: Protection against theft • starting businesses • wish magic • breaking bad fortune

VIOLET: Restoring trust • fulfilling modest ambitions • keeping secrets • secret love

WINTERGREEN: Protection • healing • deflecting hostility • reducing debt and misfortune

WOODRUFF, SWEET: Victory in sports • career • challenges • happiness (especially in LGBTQ+ relationships)

Vanilla

4

MAGICAL COOKERY

COOKING WITH fruits, vegetables, herbs, and spices is a highly accessible form of plant magic. Everyday ingredients from grocery stores or farmers' markets can empower kitchen table and stovetop spells, blending magic with the practicality of cooking. Cooking and spellcasting are naturally intertwined, both involving processes that channel intention, like chopping, stirring, and mixing.

Whether preparing a simple dish or an elaborate feast, focus on calm, positive energy. If stressed, stick to easy recipes or soothing tasks like stirring to avoid transferring negative emotions into your meal.

Meals connected to ancestors, especially from old recipe books or on special days like the Day of the Ancestors on November 1, can invite blessings and even their comforting presence. Magical cookery is about intention, not culinary skill; a store-bought cake can be just as powerful when infused with love and topped with wish-carrying candles.

Empower ingredients, utensils, and cooking spaces by passing your hands clockwise above them while invoking health, happiness, and abundance. Call on household angels like Jophiel for blessings, Isda for nourishment, or Seheiah for kitchen safety.

Foods' magical properties often reflect their origins: for example, grounding root vegetables differ from energizing tropical spices. Let intuition guide you in infusing magic into every meal you create.

Empowering Ingredients for Magical Cookery

Fruits, nuts, and seeds are central to food magic, especially if they are eaten raw, because the pure life force will rapidly flow to activate the purpose. Cooking allows for matters to develop in their own time. To empower these ingredients, hold unpeeled fruits or vegetables in your hand or place nuts or seeds in a dish (or, if easier, between your open-cupped hands). Before adding them to the recipe or eating them directly, name the power of the ingredient plus the specific intention and desired timeframe for that intention to manifest upon consumption.

If your ingredient has inedible seeds, stones, shells, cores, peels, or the like, these can be buried after eating the food item, representing the ongoing fulfillment of your need or desire. If a need is more urgent, they can be cast into running water. If you are eating something without seeds or the like, a few uneaten pieces can be substituted. For extra spell power, a wish to be fulfilled or a representation of what is to be lost can be scratched invisibly with the index finger of the writing hand or scored with a sharp knife on the skin or peel of a fruit or vegetable before burying it or casting it into flowing water.

For banishing whomever or whatever you wish to lose from your life, bury a decaying fruit and allow it to bring new life or love in its own time. Nuts are a common fertility symbol, as are berries, both for conceiving a child and launching any creative venture or business. Keep fresh, shareable fruit on hand that you have blessed, such as golden apples or grapes, to circulate the life force; offer a selection to visitors to spread health and abundance. Endow fruit in a child's, teen's, or partner's lunchbox with whatever strengths or protection they need during the day. Finally, if you are on vacation and want to try local produce that is not in the list below, assess whether it is watery or spicy and the kind of dishes in which it is used to divine the energetic properties of the ingredient.

Elemental Powers

I have added the elements associated with each ingredient on the following list, whether offering the powers of the secure Earth; the logical and focused Air; the inspirational/protective Fire; or the empathic, intuitive, people-centered Water. This enables you to balance the elemental mix in any environment or situation by offering relevant foods or to modify your own feelings by eating a certain ingredient.

Magical Meanings of · PLANT-BASED INGREDIENTS ·

ACAI BERRY

ELEMENT: Air

MAGICAL COOKERY: Popularly used in drinks, as puree, smoothies, and health bars • protection by Archangel Michael • opening possibilities thought unattainable

ALFALFA SPROUT

ELEMENT: Water

MAGICAL COOKERY: Increasing income or resources (when eaten during the waxing moon) • staving off debt or financial loss (when eaten during the waning moon)

ALMOND

ELEMENT: Air

MAGICAL COOKERY: Attracting money • commitment in love • fertility • maintaining prosperity • wisdom

APPLE

ELEMENTS: Water, Earth

MAGICAL COOKERY: Fertility, especially to conceive a boy • initiating creative ideas and ventures • love • health • long life and youthfulness • vitality • regeneration

APRICOT

ELEMENT: Water

MAGICAL COOKERY: Abundance and fertility • charisma • the power to grant wishes • mending love rifts • increasing self-esteem

ARUGULA (AKA ROCKET)

ELEMENT: Fire

MAGICAL COOKERY: Wise financial investments • aphrodisiac, especially combined with tomatoes

ASPARAGUS

ELEMENT: Air

MAGICAL COOKERY: Potency (aphrodisiac) • attraction of money when dipped into a prosperity herb sauce (for example, basil-based)

AVOCADO

ELEMENTS: Water, Earth

MAGICAL COOKERY: Sensuality • inner radiance and outer charisma • promoting well-being on all levels • attracting beautiful things and luxury into your life

BANANA

ELEMENT: Water

MAGICAL COOKERY: Fertility • male potency • prosperity • love and fulfillment in the middle years • safety while traveling • should not be cut, only broken

BEAN

ELEMENTS: Earth, Air

MAGICAL COOKERY: Removing illness • increasing male sexual potency • enchanting a lover (without interfering with free will) • protection against malice (good if difficult relatives or neighbors are calling)

BEAN, GREEN

ELEMENT: Air

MAGICAL COOKERY: Attracting money • growth in new ventures • uniting people at a shared meal or celebration

BEAN, LIMA/BUTTER (ESPECIALLY LARGE ONES)

ELEMENT: Air

MAGICAL COOKERY: Mending quarrels between a couple • reducing stress • bringing abundance and prosperity, particularly if shelled from the pod • speckled ones: aiding networking

BEANSPROUT

ELEMENT: Water

MAGICAL COOKERY: Networking and bringing together new family members with existing ones • acquiring money in numerous small amounts

BILBERRY

ELEMENT: Water

MAGICAL COOKERY: Increasing clairvoyant sight • protection against and removal of hexes and ill-wishing when eaten

BLUEBERRY

ELEMENT: Water

MAGICAL COOKERY: Protection against psychic or psychological attack (whether eaten raw, taken as tea or cooked, especially on full moon) • family celebrations

BROCCOLI

ELEMENT: Water

MAGICAL COOKERY: Gaining and maintaining a steady source of income • protection if you are overgenerous or underappreciated

BRUSSELS SPROUT

ELEMENT: Water

MAGICAL COOKERY: Inflow of money by the next full moon (if steamed or lightly cooked during the three days before or on the day of the full moon) • unification of the family over a contentious issue (if seasoned) • need for extra effort to break through fixed opinions (if served to you overcooked)

CAPER

ELEMENT: Fire

MAGICAL COOKERY: Aphrodisiac for male potency • attracting good luck and unmasking those who would deceive

CARROT

ELEMENT: Fire

MAGICAL COOKERY: Female fertility and male potency (aphrodisiac) • improves clairvoyance • increases motivation

CAULIFLOWER

ELEMENTS: Water, Earth

MAGICAL COOKERY: Calming irritability and dramas in the home • filling the aura energy field with quiet assurance (when eaten before facing a challenging situation or environment)

CHERRY

ELEMENT: Water

MAGICAL COOKERY: New or young love • growing trust • increasing divinatory abilities • fertility • good long-term results from small beginnings

CHICKPEA (AKA GARBANZO)

ELEMENT: Earth

MAGICAL COOKERY: Overcoming competition, rivals, and opposition (especially by those who use unfair means) • mothering in all its aspects • preventing possessiveness in relationships

CHILI

ELEMENT: Fire

MAGICAL COOKERY: Inflaming passion • preventing a mate from straying • removing hexes, curses, and ill-wishes (invite the perpetrator to a chili dinner)

COCONUT

ELEMENT: Water

MAGICAL COOKERY: Fertility • motherhood • the flow of new life and energies • protection against all negativity (especially psychic attack)

CORN, SWEET

ELEMENT: Fire

MAGICAL COOKERY: Provision of what is most needed • abundance • good luck • fertility • beginning an exciting new enterprise • sacrificing short-term benefits for long-term gain

DRAGON FRUIT

ELEMENTS: Water, Fire

MAGICAL COOKERY: linked to the moon and as part of a shared feast on the full moon • all forms of dragon magic • courage and finding hidden treasure, maybe as undeveloped talents within self

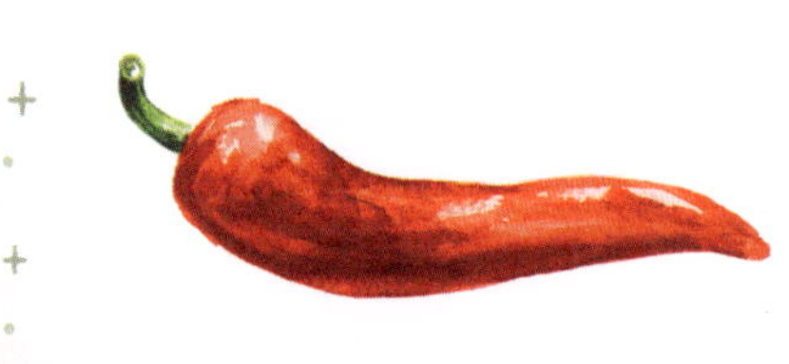

EDAMAME

ELEMENT: Fire

MAGICAL COOKERY: New ventures that will take time to develop • attracting financial backing to business ideas

EGGPLANT (AKA AUBERGINE)

ELEMENT: Earth

MAGICAL COOKERY: Abundance • gradual regrowth after loss or setback • insight into indecision • purple: courage • white: protection

FIG

ELEMENT: Fire

MAGICAL COOKERY: Birth • creativity • fertility • harmony and balance • prosperity • sensuality • wisdom

FLOUR

ELEMENT: Earth

MAGICAL COOKERY: Stable, lasting results to any needs for which the meal has been created • abundant resources (when kept in a kitchen jar that is always full) • properties can vary based on the type of grain used to make the flour

GARLIC

ELEMENT: Earth

MAGICAL COOKERY: Psychic protection, especially against unfriendly spirits and earthly intruders • calling the wise ancestors • passion • banishing harm

GINGER

ELEMENT: Fire

MAGICAL COOKERY: Whatever you need urgently • fiercely defensive • bringing or renewing passion

GRAPE

ELEMENTS: Water, Air

MAGICAL COOKERY: Commitment in love • good luck in games of chance • a better lifestyle • joy • ecstasy • rebirth • renewal • transformation • passion

HAZELNUT

ELEMENT: Air

MAGICAL COOKERY: Fertility • knowledge and wisdom • happy long-term commitment • justice (personal and official)

HEART OF PALM

ELEMENT: Water

MAGICAL COOKERY: Fertility • potency • energy • starting again • rejuvenation

HONEY, FLOWER

ELEMENT: Fire

MAGICAL COOKERY: Abundance • creativity • hospitality • a welcoming home • fertility • health • prosperity • whatever is most desired • nurturing • maternal power and wisdom • properties vary according to the flower from which it is collected

HUCKLEBERRY

ELEMENT: Water

MAGICAL COOKERY: Protection and a strong connection with nature and nature spirits • increased intuition and awareness of the unseen

KALE

ELEMENT: Fire

MAGICAL COOKERY: Courage • determination • fighting against injustice • sporting prowess and stamina

KIWI

ELEMENTS: Water, Earth

MAGICAL COOKERY: Unconditional love • opening the heart to new family members • tolerance • forgiveness of self as well as others

LEMON

ELEMENT: Water

MAGICAL COOKERY: Cleansing quarrels, misunderstandings, and harsh words • encouraging clarity of thought • overcoming addictions and destructive ties from the past • travel and house moves

LENTIL

ELEMENT: Earth

MAGICAL COOKERY: Harmonious, leisurely family meals (if your family or partner usually graze or rush in and out) • defusing intergenerational conflicts

LETTUCE

ELEMENT: Water

MAGICAL COOKERY: Advantage in a situation (the stronger the leaves, the more you will gain) • money (eat on full moon day or night for a bonus or chance to make a one-off source of money)

LIME

ELEMENT: Water

MAGICAL COOKERY: Justice • new beginnings • new places and people, fresh investment and original ideas • to repel spite and jealousy

MANGO

ELEMENT: Water

MAGICAL COOKERY: Health • stability in career • lasting happiness • for wise home or vehicle purchases

MELON, HONEYDEW

ELEMENT: Water

MAGICAL COOKERY: Reset for body and mind • ideal for mornings • stress release and mood boost • overcoming sluggishness • addictions

MUSHROOM

ELEMENT: Earth

MAGICAL COOKERY: Avoiding illusion and those who would deceive • contact with nature spirits (especially on May Eve, Midsummer, and Halloween)

NUT, BRAZIL

ELEMENT: Fire

MAGICAL COOKERY: Good luck token (particularly in love) • building authority and prestige for a major move forward or promotion (eat a few a day) • formal learning • only eat the processed nut

NUT, CASHEW (PEELED)

ELEMENT: Fire

MAGICAL COOKERY: Job applications and interviews • socializing • networking gatherings

NUT, MACADAMIA

ELEMENT: Fire

MAGICAL COOKERY: Youthfulness and improved memory in later years • positive body image • physical, psychological, and psychic protection, as it is the toughest nut in the world to crack open to eat • refusal to abandon principles

ONION

ELEMENT: Fire

MAGICAL COOKERY: Protection of the home, like garlic hung on strings in the kitchen • overcoming sickness, obsessions, fears, and addictions by etching the name of the affliction on the outer onion skin and burying it before cooking the remaining onion

PARSNIP

ELEMENT: Fire

MAGICAL COOKERY: Protection against debt • throw peelings away on a compost heap or outdoors food bin to remove any money drains from the home and eat the cooked parsnips to draw in money

PASSIONFRUIT

ELEMENT: Water

MAGICAL COOKERY: Finding love at first sight • dreams of your lover or the person you will meet who will inflame your heart • passion for a creative interest or performing art that overrides all other priorities

PEA

ELEMENT: Air

MAGICAL COOKERY: Business and money-spinning opportunities (shelled) • enhancing charisma and the ability to attract whom and what you want into your sphere (raw) • resolution of small worries and calling small benefits and favors (cooked; the last spoonful is especially lucky for small wins)

PEA, BLACK-EYED

ELEMENT: Air

MAGICAL COOKERY: Increasing clairvoyant vision • protect against the evil eye and spite

PEACH

ELEMENT: Water

MAGICAL COOKERY: Attracting beautiful artifacts • inner beauty and radiance • becoming a femme fatale • marriage • pregnancy • a healthy birth • long life

PEANUT (AKA GROUNDNUT)

ELEMENTS: Earth, Fire

MAGICAL COOKERY: Financial growth from small beginnings or over a period of time • sociability and networking at gatherings

PEAR

ELEMENTS: Earth, Water

MAGICAL COOKERY: New life • health • girls' and women's needs and rituals • fertility • conception of a girl

PEPPERS (RED, GREEN, YELLOW)

ELEMENT: Fire

MAGICAL COOKERY: Increasing courage • extra strength and stamina • assisting in remaining calm • protection

PINEAPPLE

ELEMENTS: Fire, Water

MAGICAL COOKERY: Obtaining the resources for a major purchase (a scoop or two of dried and finely chopped rind left over from preparing the fruit for consumption, carried in a money sachet) • striving for a luxury lifestyle • endowing good fortune and creating a bond among all who share a cake into which pineapple has been baked

PLUM

ELEMENT: Water

MAGICAL COOKERY: Novelty and exciting change (eat three plums and carry the washed stones in a charm bag) • quelling anxiety over being good at parenthood (share or bake plum pie for a lover)

POMEGRANATE

ELEMENT: Water

MAGICAL COOKERY: Unexpected wealth • seed: divination (keep the seeds after preparation and ask a yes/no question, using the seeds to count for the answer) • juice: magical ink for writing petitions and instead of blood in ancient spells with equal effect and more ethically

POTATO

ELEMENT: Earth

MAGICAL COOKERY: Building up opportunity step by step • perseverance • long-term security • valuing simple pleasures and good-hearted people who may not seem exciting

PUMPKIN

ELEMENT: Earth

MAGICAL COOKERY: Protection from all malevolent spirits • unity if family loyalties are questioned (pumpkin pies welcome all to the table)

RADISH

ELEMENT: Fire

MAGICAL COOKERY: Protection against the evil eye • aphrodisiac • do not give to potentially volatile people or those quick to take offense

RASPBERRY

ELEMENT: Water

MAGICAL COOKERY: Tea or fruit: speeding slow-moving matters where others are being obstructive or using delaying tactics

RHUBARB

ELEMENT: Earth

MAGICAL COOKERY: Fidelity (when baked in pies or stewed) • aphrodisiac if a man has been made to doubt his virility • happy family

RICE

ELEMENTS: Earth, Water

MAGICAL COOKERY: Prosperity • marital happiness • fertility • keep a rice jar topped up in the kitchen to draw prosperity and happiness to daily life

RICE, SWEET (AKA GLUTINOUS, STICKY)

ELEMENTS: Earth, Fire

MAGICAL COOKERY: Romance • domestic happiness • harmonious family gatherings • always enough food, fuel, and clothing for the year ahead

SPINACH

ELEMENTS: Air, Water

MAGICAL COOKERY: Stamina and perseverance to push through necessary but unwelcome situations • swift and satisfactory resolution of challenges

SQUASH, WINTER

ELEMENTS: Water, Air

MAGICAL COOKERY: Protection against restless spirits and hyperactive people who stir up chaos • solid resources rather than immense wealth

STRAWBERRY

ELEMENT: Water

MAGICAL COOKERY: Shared with a lover: romance, flirtations, fun, and enchantment • made into or bought as jelly or jam: sweetening any occasion and bringing laughter

SWEET POTATO/YAM

ELEMENTS: Earth, Water

MAGICAL COOKERY: Connecting with your roots, ancestors, and family • sweetens friendship and kinship bonds that may have become distant

TANGERINE/MANDARIN

ELEMENT: Fire

MAGICAL COOKERY: Faithful love • increased commitment or marriage • prosperity • good fortune • increased passion

within an established relationship that may have lost its spark

TOMATO

ELEMENT: Water

MAGICAL COOKERY: On the window ledge: health • on a shelf near heat or a fireplace: prosperity • eaten raw: fertility, health, and abundance

TOFU (AKA SOY/SOYA)

ELEMENTS: Fire, Earth

MAGICAL COOKERY: Soy sauce: protection of finances and love life • use soy/tofu in meals: overcoming challenges and embracing opportunities if your life path is taking another direction

TURNIP

ELEMENT: Earth

MAGICAL COOKERY: Gentle ending, whether involving a relationship or any natural transition such as retirement (cooked)

UGLI FRUIT

ELEMENT: Earth

MAGICAL COOKERY: Defiance of any who have tried to make you feel inferior or unattractive • making public hidden talents • success that puts any detractor in their place

WHEAT

ELEMENT: Earth

MAGICAL COOKERY: Fulfillment of what was started six months earlier • successful completion of projects • long-term gains • successful property transactions, renovation, or redecoration

WILD CARROT (AKA QUEEN ANNE'S LACE)

ELEMENT: Fire

MAGICAL COOKERY: Increased sexual desire • releasing inhibitions

ZUCCHINI (AKA COURGETTE)

ELEMENT: Air

MAGICAL COOKERY: Preserving fidelity (etch your love's name on the side of a zucchini and cook it) • Preventing unfaithfulness (freeze the zucchini containing their name)

CONCLUSION

Here the book ends and your personal journey through the magical world of plants begins. I have suggested ways you can use plants to attract what you need and desire most and to keep away harm. However, you will already have your own family-favorite herbs and remedies and will no doubt create more to pass on to future generations.

Go now where there are flowers or plant your flower meadow in a spare patch of garden. Buy a beautiful potted plant if you live in a cramped apartment and inhale its fragrance and its magic. Recall that the world is beautiful and that you can walk in that beauty manifest by the plant world, even in a city square.

As I stand in my suburban garden in the rain and absorb the magic, I send you my blessings.

Cassandra Eason
July 2025

ACKNOWLEDGMENTS

My deepest thanks to John Gold—my subeditor, protector, and mentor—and to Kornelia Gold, my inspiration and wonderful friend. I am sincerely grateful to Kate Zimmermann, former executive editor at Union Square & Co., who kept faith with me throughout the many years I have written for Sterling/Union Square & Co. Finally, very special thanks to executive editor Barbara Berger, project editor Kristin Mandaglio, interior designer and cover art director Stacy Forte, production manager Terence Campo, and cover and chapter opener illustrator Eleanor Taylor.

PICTURE CREDITS

Eleanor Taylor: cover, 10–11, 50–51, 84–85, 118–119

Getty Images: achtung_ein (125), Alina Firsova (109), Anastasiia Eroshova (55), arxichtu4ki (9, 36), bartol_art (110, 123), BarvArt (134), Daria Ustiugova (6, 19, 41, 73, 77, 102, 126, 128, 134), dvoriankin (87), Ekaterina Kudriavtseva (78), Ekaterina Lanbina (113), Elena Bragina (17, 122, 133), Elena Medvedeva (12, 56, 81), Elena Smirnova (61), Evgeniia Babanova (6, 76), Evgeniya Ivanova (21, 44), Farida Biktimirova (142), Hanna Tsishkevich (34), Illustrator Vector Artist (131), Inna Sinano (139), Irina Zemskova (138), ivan-96 (127, 140), Jana Salnikova (83), katsiaryna martsinenka (29, 73), L Feddes (18), Leyla Özcan (23, 124), LightFieldStudios (79), Marina Skryzhova, (26), Natalia Kunashova (68, 90), Natalia Plyashkevich (33), Nataliia Sumina (62), Nelli Andrieieva (14), OGri (129), Ola_Tarakanova (61), Olga Ivanova (47), photo_iget (25), PJ_nice (70), satika (91), Svitlana Khlivna (80, 136), Tatiana Khramtsova (42, 99), vector_ann (130), VVadyab (66)

Shutterstock.com: a.designer (43), ARTBRUSH (20), Design 35 (31), EleniKa (93), farfalla813 (32), Farzanak (22, 82, 137), Gringoann.art (117), Here (background), lera lysenko (38), losmosX (107), Maria_09 (53, 65), mutia_paint (54), Nikiparonak (59), Ola-la (24), Retropix (17), TrendyTees Studio (45)

ABOUT THE AUTHOR

CASSANDRA EASON is a prolific author, writing on all aspects of spirituality and magic, in addition to lecturing, broadcasting, and facilitating workshops throughout the world. During the past forty years Cassandra has written more than 130 titles, many of which have been translated into numerous languages, including Japanese, Russian, Hebrew, Portuguese, German, Dutch, and Spanish.

Among her bestsellers are *A Spell a Day*, *A Little Bit of Palmistry*, *The Complete Book of Women's Wisdom*, and *The Modern Day Druidess*, to name just a few. In the 1001 series, Cassandra has written *1001 Magical Plants*, *1001 Spells*, *1001 Dreams*, *1001 Tarot Spreads*, and *1001 Crystals*.

Her books have been serialized in publications around the world, including the *Daily Mail*, the *Daily Mirror*, the *Daily Express*, *People*, *The Sun*, *News of the World* magazine, *Spirit and Destiny*, *Fate and Fortune*, *Prediction*, *Best and Bella*, *Homes and Gardens*, *Good Housekeeping*, and *Woman's Day* (Australia).

In the UK, Cassandra had her own weekly miniseries, *Sixth Sense*, and she was the resident presenter for over two years on *Psychic Live Time*. She acted as a psychic consultant and expert on the successful ITV *Magic and Mystery* series and has also analyzed dreams on the UK's Channel 4 *Big Brother* seasons 3 and 4 and *Celebrity Big Brother*.